Puffin Books
THE PUFFIN B

From its early days as a pastime for bored monks, tennis has become a fascinating game for players and spectators of all ages. Originally considered a genteel sport, it is now as businesslike and professional as any of the other major world sports.

As Chief Sports Writer on the *Sunday Times* for many years, Brian Glanville is well qualified to trace the origins of the game and examine the development of tennis from the days of gentle amateurism to the big-time professionalism we're familiar with today.

In this book you can read about the top players who have moulded the game into its present form – names that have thrilled, angered and inspired: early stars such as the Doherty brothers, Suzanne Lenglen and Jean Borotra, the charismatic Fred Perry and Jack Kramer, the tragic Little Mo, and super-stars Rod Laver, Billie Jean King and Bjorn Borg.

Whether armchair enthusiasts or budding champions, readers of twelve upwards will find this book compulsive reading.

THE PUFFIN BOOK OF
TENNIS
BRIAN GLANVILLE

Puffin Books

Puffin Books, Penguin Books Ltd, Harmondsworth, Middlesex, England
Penguin Books, 625 Madison Avenue, New York, New York 10022, U.S.A.
Penguin Books Australia Ltd, Ringwood, Victoria, Australia
Penguin Books Canada Ltd, 2801 John Street, Markham,
Ontario, Canada L3R 1B4
Penguin Books (N.Z.) Ltd, 182–190 Wairau Road, Auckland 10, New Zealand

First published 1981

Made and printed in Great Britain by
Richard Clay (The Chaucer Press) Ltd, Bungay, Suffolk
Set in Linotype Baskerville

Contents

Beginnings

It was probably inevitable that tennis, sooner or later, would move out of doors. The wonder of it was that it took so long to do so: the better part of eight hundred years. Though all sorts of exotic claims and all sorts of bizarre explanations have been made and given for its origins, there seems not much doubt that its true ancestor was the French game, *jeu de paume*, devised by monks in the cloisters of twelfth-century monasteries, while its modern form, lawn tennis, sprang from the fertile brain of an English Victorian.

How could it not? The Victorians, after all, were the true inventors of modern sport. They gave the world soccer and rugby; even the current version of athletics. Schoolboys at heart, they were forever – like those medieval monks – thinking up new, ingenious diversions.

To those Victorians, personifications of the sporting spirit and true amateurs, the contemporary tennis world would appear almost as foreign as it would to those medieval monks. During the 1970s the game waxed and proliferated at almost dizzy speed. Professionalism, which for years had been no more than an enclave, a kind of travelling circus – even if its members outstripped any amateur – now ran riot. Players like Bjorn Borg and Jimmy Connors could become millionaires. Massive prizes were to be won at comparatively obscure tournaments. Women players, so long spurned, were themselves able to earn sums to make the wealthiest professional soccer player blink. Challenge matches between the leading male players were played for massive stakes in such neon-lit places as Las Vegas. The vast Houston Astrodome in Texas was thronged by a crowd anxious to see Billie Jean King, the queen of American tennis, play the veteran Bobby Riggs, who had derided the prowess of women players.

It is said that the original game of tennis was developed by bored monks of junior status, and that the first balls were made of monks' old habits. I do not think we should take too seriously the claim that tennis began in Egypt in the Nile delta town of Tammis or Tinnis, or that it originated in Ancient Greece, where Nausicaa and her maidens played it, or that the Persians, the Indians of Mexico or the Saracens were its begetters, though it is true that the word 'racquet' is of Arabic origin, meaning the palm of the hand.

It seems likely that the French imperative *tenez* – meaning 'Play!' – was the word which gave birth to 'tennis'; in English, the word was first known as 'tenetz'. Real tennis is quite clearly the descendant of that strange game which the monks played among themselves – an indoor sport where the court was full of strange hazards, buttresses and embrasures which plainly had their origin in the cloisters where the monks developed it.

Lawn tennis largely took over the scoring method of the original game. That strange progression from 'love' to 'game' through fifteen, thirty and forty is directly derived from real tennis, though 'forty-five' has been diminished to 'forty'. It has been suggested that the obsession with the number sixty in the Middle Ages was at the root of this strange way of scoring which followed the clock. This might be sufficient explanation in itself, though it has also been mooted that the French bet money on the game in multiples of fifteen, reflecting their coinage system at the time. The word 'love' is just as elusive. Does it derive from *l'œuf* (the egg), the shape of which imperfectly suggests a zero, or are its origins in English rather than French, love being an intangible quality? Who knows?

'Deuce', when the opponents are level at forty-all, is easier to understand. It is a corruption of *deux*, the French word for 'two', denoting that it takes two more points to win the game.

It has been thought that lawn tennis may have had its origins at Hampton Court where a real tennis court used by kings has long stood. Those waiting on the lawns outside would amuse themselves by hitting a tennis ball around. Perhaps. What we do know is that a rudimentary kind of lawn tennis was played in the sixteenth century, for the delight of Queen Elizabeth I, by servants of the Earl of Hertford in Somerset. The French also developed a game called long tennis – hitting a cork ball over a mound – which seems to have caught on in England in the late eighteenth century. Sheer speculation, again. We had better get down to brass tacks and introduce Major Gem, Clerk to the Birmingham Magistrates, who with his friend Perera, a Spaniard, was playing a kind of lawn tennis in the 1860s. The widely diffused playing of croquet saw to it that Victorians of some substance already had the lawns to play on. In 1872 Gem, Perera and a couple

of local doctors set up the first lawn tennis club in
Leamington Spa at the Manor House Hotel.

It was a Major Wingfield, however, who applied to
patent the game of lawn tennis a couple of years later,
and who is generally regarded as the game's inventor.
By chance – or perhaps by some obscure design – John
Wingfield, the major's ancestor, had gaoled Charles
of Orleans, grandson of a king of France and a tennis
player, after the Battle of Agincourt in 1415. That
other major, Gem, seems to have beaten him by at
least a year as Wingfield did not begin the game he
first called Sphairistiké till 1873 at a country house
party in Wales – a Christmas diversion.

One of its strangest features was that Wingfield
thought it might be played not only on grass but on
ice. The court described the shape of an hour-glass,
the net dipped in the middle from 5 feet to 4 feet 8
inches and the sidelines and baseline each measured
30 feet. There was a diamond-shaped serving crease on
one side and a service line on the other. Scoring was
the same as in rackets, with fifteen points per game,
more if the players found themselves at thirteen or
fourteen-all. Significantly, Major Wingfield described
it as a 'portable court for playing the ancient game of
tennis'.

Although the British Lawn Tennis Association has
called Major Wingfield the inventor of lawn tennis,
it is probably closer to the mark – as we have seen – to
regard him as a resourceful opportunist. In one form or
another, the game had clearly been around for some
time. It did not find favour with everybody, though
the criticisms of it were curiously contradictory. Given
the behaviour on court of such passionate performers
as Nastase, Connors, McEnroe, Navratilova, and even

Virginia Wade, it is interesting to see that some con-
demned it because it did not encourage team spirit.
Others, however, disliked it because they saw it as
a mere social diversion, fit chiefly for women (they
could scarcely have visualized our Kings, Austins and
Navratilovas!) and never to be taken seriously or
practised.

The hour-glass court, which may to a degree have
been suggested to Wingfield by the strange shape of
the real tennis court, was clearly not long for this
world. Curiously, the Marylebone Cricket Club, who
at first staked a claim in this new territory, supported
the hour-glass court in 1875. That, however, was the
year in which the All England Croquet Club began to
play tennis, and the days of the M.C.C.'s control were
numbered. In 1877 the *Field* magazine, which had
played a lively part in encouraging the new sport, put
up a twenty-five-guinea cup to be competed for at the
All England Club, Wimbledon. A sub-committee,
chaired by Major Heathcote, was appointed to modify
the rules. He was assisted by Mr Jones, who had promoted the game at the club, and Mr Marshall, the
club secretary, a great expert on sports played with a
racket.

What they decided and devised has endured astonishingly long and well. The court now became a rect-
angle, 78 by 27 feet. The net was lowered to 3 feet
3 inches at the centre, the service line was to be 26 feet
from the net. It was as early as this, moreover, that
the game was weighted so markedly in favour of the
server. He was to be permitted a second service, if his
first were faulty.

Was it right? Is it right? The player who serves is
already at a massive advantage, even though Heathcote

and company could not have envisaged the wicked, immensely rapid, devilishly swerving services of such as John McEnroe. Giving a server two services meant not only that he had a double chance of success, but that he or she could take risks on the first service, going for maximum pace, knowing that a second chance remained if the serve went wrong. At this stage, it is clear enough that the rules are never going to be changed, but the practice remains a controversial one.

This first Wimbledon was so much a server's tournament that something had to be done. The next year it duly was; the service line was moved four feet closer to a net which had yet to find its ideal height. The first of all Wimbledon champions, Spencer Gore, lived on his volleying; a practice allegedly discovered by a Mr Woodhouse. Gore explained that his opponents, most of them brought up on real tennis, hit the ball back in a way which made volleying very easy. It is interesting that from so early in the history of the game serve and volley tactics carried the day, even if they were clearly a gentle affair by comparison with the ferocious game we now know, a game which so often makes rallies brief and brutal, and which has caused some to prefer as a spectacle the women's game, with its gentler, more protracted rallies.

That volleying, like the game, was very much in its infancy was shown the next year when Hadow, the winner, overcame Gore's volleying by simply lobbing the ball over his or any other would-be volleyer's head, sending them scampering back to retrieve the ball, and finally exhausting them. 'Pat ball!' sneered Gore. Still, rudimentary though such tactics were, they represented the first successful attempt to beat the volleyer at other than his own game. One must, however, make it clear that Spencer Gore, fine player of racket games and great innovator though he was, was accustomed to hit the ball on the volley *before* it crossed the net and reached his side of the court – a practice which would be outlawed in 1880. In these circumstances, the achievement of P. Frank Hadow in beating him was all the greater.

Gore, a natural athlete who had been a fine player of racket games at his public school, Harrow, was very mobile, with a powerful, flexible wrist. He adapted his game to the conditions imposed by the net of that time; it was no less than 5 feet high at the posts, making passing shots – shots which pass the player at the net – virtually impossible.

A true tennis style was still to be achieved, however. It was inevitable that players should bring with them to the new sport the techniques they had learned in the older racket games; a heavy emphasis on flicks of the wrist in rackets, a stiff wrist and a preference for cutting and slicing the ball from real tennis. Then, in 1879, came the Renshaw brothers, Ernest and William, and the game was transformed. There are those who feel that the Renshaws, rather than Gore, were the true pioneers of the serve and volley game.

The Renshaws were entered for the Wimbledon tournament of 1879 – on the lawns, as it is picturesquely said, of the All England Club – but cannily, they did not compete; they merely and shrewdly watched the others.

The following year they entered for the newly inaugurated doubles championship, played, as it would be till 1884, not at Wimbledon but at Oxford University. This they won, as they did the following year, when William also won the singles title. It was then the fashion – as it would be for so long in the international Davis Cup – to have a tournament whose winner then qualified to meet the champion in a so-called challenge round. This William duly won against the holder, J. T. Hartley. He proceeded to win the next five titles in a row, in all collecting seven, and would doubtless have won in 1887 and 1888, had it not been for attacks of what has come to be known as 'tennis elbow'. This at least allowed his brother Ernest to take a title, since he was thrice beaten by William in the challenge round.

William was small but immensely quick and highly tenacious. Like his brother, he struck the ball forcefully and low, made extensive use of the volley, and perfected the smash – the overhead 'kill' shot which put any weak, high-bouncing return ruthlessly away. Such tactics were calculated to destroy the wiles of those who hugged the baseline and tried to prevail by long, steady rallies. Note that William was able to play such a game despite a lack of height and size. Tennis, for all the vast emphasis that has been placed in modern times on serve and volleying, and the consequent premium on tall, powerful players with long reach, has remained essentially democratic in a physical sense. Bobby Riggs, who won Wimbledon in 1939 and was a match for any player of his era, was a little man. So were the two marvellous Australians who emerged after the Second World War, Ken Rosewall, ironically nicknamed 'Muscles', and the red-headed, left-handed perfectionist, Rod Laver. Touch, mobility, anticipation and morale have always been able to compensate for indifferent physique.

The closest call William Renshaw had in a Wimbledon final was in 1889 when he was playing H. S. Barlow, who had reached match point. Renshaw served fast, then dashed for the net, as boldly as any contemporary Californian. But he slipped, fell, and his racket spun out of his hand. Barlow had the whole court open to him, the title at his mercy, but through some strange aberration which he was never able to explain, he decided to lob. Perhaps the idea of unseating the great champion was simply too much for him. At all events, Renshaw was able to scramble to his feet, racket now in hand, retrieve the shot, win the point, and go on to keep the championship. Alas, both brothers died young – Ernest in 1899, William, at the age of forty-three, in 1904.

In 1882 the net, which was 4 feet high at the posts, came down to $3\frac{1}{2}$ feet: a boon to ground stroke players such as Lawford. Note that the modification took place after discussions between the All England Club and the M.C.C., who still had a finger in the pie. There was great rivalry between Lawford, whose view it was that 'perfect back-play will beat perfect volleying', and the Renshaws. When Lawford eventually took the championship in 1887, beating Ernest Renshaw in the final, he was thirty-six years old. His philosophy was that if he lost a point to a volley he had only himself to blame. The service line was now 21 feet from the net, where of course it has remained, and the overarm service, which A. T. Myers introduced in 1878, was common to virtually all male players.

By the late nineteenth century hard or clay courts, initially comprised of rolled earth, were common. As a writer observed early in the following century, there was nothing like a good grass court, but they were as rare as an auk's egg. Grass, which the ball came off more quickly, obviously favoured a more adventurous and aggressive game. Clay courts favoured a more patient style, one based on relentless slicing and top-spin – excelled at in our own time by the Swede, Bjorn Borg.

The ball, made of vulcanized rubber covered with cloth, has not seen many fundamental changes, though it did become harder in the 1930s, thereby favouring the fast servers.

The Wimbledon tournament itself had gathered popularity with phenomenal speed, not least thanks to the epic meetings of Lawford and the Renshaws. There were only 200 spectators for the first Wimbledon, but in 1885, when Lawford lost to William Renshaw, there were no fewer than 3,500 for the challenge round.

After the Renshaws, there were the Dohertys. By comparison with the halcyon 1880s, the nineties, in terms of tennis, were not gay at all until the emergence of the Doherty brothers, Big Do and Little Do, Reggie and Laurie, in the last few years of the decade. Not only were the brothers splendid players, dominating Wimbledon and the game at large, but they were also flawless sportsmen. The odd thing about Big Do, born in 1874, a couple of years before his brother, was that he was a permanent martyr to indigestion. Six feet 1 inch tall, he weighed only just over 10 stone (63 kg). 'I don't know what it is like to feel really well,' the poor fellow once said.

This did not prevent him from winning Wimbledon four years in a row, from 1897 to 1900. He had no special strength, being, by the standards of his time, completely versatile. It did not matter to Little Do either whether he played on grass, or on the slower hard courts which had already come into being. He exceeded even his elder brother's achievement, winning the Wimbledon championship five consecutive years, from 1902 to 1906. He was a super volleyer, and a very clever strategist. In 1903 he won the United States singles title and with his brother won eight major doubles championships.

Nor was their athletic prowess confined to the tennis court. Little Do, always very fast, was a sprinter and high jumper at school, and later – having given up tournament tennis – became a golfer with a plus two handicap. Big Do himself got down to scratch in golf.

Their retirement from major tennis was an odd one, but not without parallel. Their anxious mother made them do it, just as an anxious mother was responsible for the retirement from soccer of those muscular England full-backs of the same epoch, the Walters brothers. It is said that Mrs Doherty was appalled to see a doubles match, the final of the 1906 Wimbledon championship, in which the opposition, S. H. Smith and F. L. Riseley, banged the ball continually at Big Do. His mother was frightened he would be killed, so the Prince Charmings of tennis, as they were called, withdrew from serious doubles competition. Big Do was only thirty-six when he died, and Little Do but forty-three.

The Americans, who would play so large a part in the development and subsequent history of the game, already had their own national championship in 1881. Two years later C. M. and J. S. Clark, who had never been beaten in their own country, left America to play against the Renshaw brothers at Wimbledon, and lost.

In 1897 the Americans invited a British team to visit them, but none went. Three years later they proposed an international tournament for a cup put up by one of their players, a Mr Dwight Filley Davis, then a young undergraduate at Harvard. So the celebrated Davis Cup was born.

The actual donor of the cup was Davis's father, and the idea had come to the Harvard man the previous year when he travelled across the United States to represent the east against the west. The east won with ease – times would change – but Davis was so impressed by the good fellowship of the occasion that he suggested to the United States Lawn Tennis Association that the cup be instituted. It was called the Davis Cup by the captain of the eastern team, George Wright. The Americans won the first version in Boston 3–0, against a British team which did not include the unbeatable Dohertys. Tennis, so early in the twentieth century, was well and truly under way.

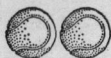

Tennis Conquers the World

It is worth dwelling on the first of those Davis Cup tournaments, if only to appreciate how rudimentary it was. It was played at a place called the Longwood Cricket Club: a reminder that the United States was the first of all countries outside Britain to take to cricket – indeed, the first ever to play host to an M.C.C. tour. Rain soaked the courts and delayed the matches, but when they were played the Americans, for whom Davis was a winner both in singles and doubles, were much too good for the English team. Their devastatingly sliced services time and again outwitted the English players. There should have been a couple more games, but with Davis leading A. S. Gore 9–7, 9–9 and looking very tired, the match came abruptly to an end, since the competitors had promised to take part in a tournament in Southampton.

Davis, later to be Governor of the Philippines and Secretary of State for War, was an idealist who believed that winning was less important than taking part. He wanted the cup named after his family to promote the friendship of nations. Cracks in the façade were to be discerned, however, even as early as this. One of the English players, H. Roper Barrett, who played in the doubles, remarked, 'The ground was abominable. The grass was long. Picture to yourself a court in England where the grass has been the longest you

have encountered; double the length of that grass and
you have the courts as they were at Longwood at that
time.' He was scarcely more enamoured of the nets
and posts, not to mention the umpires' chairs, which
were not the tall towers we are used to but common-
place chairs set on tables. Only the girls in the gallery
met with his approval.

For those purists who feel that lawn tennis began as
a gentlemanly sport, contested and run by idealists, it
will be disappointing to learn that even the Davis Cup,
the brainchild of the high-principled young Davis,
was stained, in its origins, by commercialism. In fact
the east–west match which inspired him to conceive
the Davis Cup was sponsored by a Californian real
estate salesman, perturbed by the fact that his pro-
perty was not selling too well, and keen to arouse
interest in the State by hook, by crook – or by tennis.

It was the Davis Cup, however, which, together
with the Wimbledon tournaments, provided the great
incentive to the development of tennis around the
world. Only for its initial four years was it confined to
Britain and the United States. In 1901 Britain was un-
able to get up a representative team to back its challenge, in 1902 they inexplicably left out Laurie
Doherty for a player called Pim and lost 3–2, but in
1903 Doherty played in both singles and doubles, and
Britain won at last. Doherty's ultimate record in the
Davis Cup was a dozen wins in a dozen matches,
singles and doubles.

So Britain at last held the cup, and in 1904 the challenge came not from the United States but from
France, Belgium and Austria. The following year, it
was Australasia's turn to enter the tournament. That
year, too, Miss Sutton, born in Britain but domiciled

in the United States, took the Wimbledon women's championship out of Britain for the first time. It had been inaugurated in 1884, and was dominated for years by Lottie Dod, a remarkable young woman who retired at the age of twenty-two to become a golfing champion, having already won the title five times.

Miss Dod was two months short of her sixteenth birthday when, in 1887, she succeeded for the first time. Scorning long skirts, she moved about the court with extraordinary speed, affecting a chic white school cap. She had learned the game in Cheshire, against male visitors to her home. Technically, she was a pioneer, being one of the first to change her grip when switching from a forehand to a backhand shot, just as she was the first woman to volley. For this stroke she used what has come to be known as the Western grip, her knuckles facing the net, imparting a degree of underspin which made the ball come off the grass court very awkwardly. Oddly, however, this young tomboy chose to serve underarm rather than overarm, believing that the overarm service was mere waste of strength.

Those were endearingly casual days. Having won the title for a second time in 1888, Miss Dod did not trouble to compete for it again till 1891, when inevitably she won it, as indeed she did by defeating a Mrs Hillyard in the finals of 1892 and 1893. It was all, however, too easy and tiresome. She retired. But what she had to say about the game, and practising for the game, was of great relevance. She strongly advocated hitting the ball against a wall for volleys as well as other shots, and hitting it after the top of its bounce – a practice generalized only in the 1960s.

Lottie Dod was an innovator, too, in her determina-

tion to keep the head of the racket always above the
wrist; again, common practice now, but by no means
so common then in a game still echoing its ancestors,
with their differing techniques. She placed great
emphasis on quick recovery and athleticism. She was
altogether ahead of her time and, in many senses, of
the men players of her time.

What, meanwhile, of the Davis Cup, that progenitor
of international tennis? In 1907 Australasia became
the third name to figure on the cup when they defeated Britain by three games to two. The star of that
Australian team, and many more to come, was the
left-handed, unvaryingly cloth-capped Sir Norman
Brookes. A slight man, Brookes compensated for his
indifferent physique with a splendid ball sense – he
was another tennis player who became an excellent
golfer. A man who kept himself rigorously fit, he was
a Davis Cup player for fifteen years, beginning his
career in 1905, when he was already twenty-eight, and
not ending it till after the First World War, in 1920.

Four years later at Wimbledon, when he was forty-
seven, he gave one of his bravest performances on No. 1
Court where, before a crowd of 6,000, he defeated
F. T. Hunter, an American who had been runner-up
the previous year, over five long sets. His volleying was
superb. Later Brookes became a stalwart of the Australian Lawn Tennis Association, whose President he
was for twenty-eight years, besides being captain and
sole selector of the Davis Cup team he himself had
graced for so long.

Tennis, as we have seen, had been quick to organize
itself. The English Lawn Tennis Association was born
as early as 1888, and combined with the All England
Club to organize the Wimbledon tournament which

has kept its allure over the years, whatever the changes and revolutions of the game. In 1913 the International Lawn Tennis Federation was set up.

The sport, indeed, had swept the world, and Australasia took a stranglehold on the Davis Cup, winning it five times in a row – though let us remember that the institution of the challenge round gave a great advantage to the holders. and the Australians did have a walk-over in 1910. Thrice they defeated the Americans, on the last two occasions achieving a clean sweep 5–0. Britain took the title back in 1912 but lost it to America the following year, the Australians regaining it in 1914, and retaining it in 1919 when the tournament was resumed after the war.

Now an extraordinary spell of dominance ensued, first by the United States, then by France, who, respectively, won the trophy no less than seven and six years in a row. It was the epoch of Tilden and Johnston, of Borotra, Cochet and Lacoste: France's Three Musketeers.

Tilden and the Musketeers

The invincible American Davis Cup team of the 1920s owed its success largely to Bill Tilden and Bill Johnston, known, rather after the fashion of the Doherty brothers, as Big Bill and Little Bill.

Even in the age of Borg, McEnroe and Connors, older experts still regard Tilden as the greatest tennis player of all time. 'Tilden,' said Fred Perry (finest of all English players), 'was the greatest ever seen. With Bill Tilden, you were always thinking. He'd always play you differently.'

The remarkable thing was that some of Tilden's best years were lost in the First World War. By 1920, when he began to overshadow world tennis, he was already twenty-seven years old. The 1930s would see tennis dominated increasingly by players from modest backgrounds. In Tilden's time, and that of the Three Musketeers, gentle birth was still no obstacle to success in tennis. The era of professionalism lay in the future. Tilden was born into a wealthy family in Philadelphia. He was always fascinated by the technique of the game, and helped to perfect his own by teaching fellow students at college. Curiously, his interest and his commitment were increased by an accident in which he lost the top of one of his right-hand fingers, which obliged him to alter his grip. This he did to astonishing purpose. His height and his physical strength were already great assets; an analyst of his game once told him that his chief power actually came from the thighs.

In 1918 and 1919 he was runner-up in the American singles championship. In 1920 he came to Wimbledon and won it for the first time. Curiously enough, he would do so only twice more, and at a remarkably long interval. Having retained it in 1921, the year before Wimbledon's grounds moved from Worple Road to Church Road, he stayed away till 1927, when he lost a bizarre semi-final to Henri Cochet. He scored his last success at the advanced age of thirty-seven, in 1930.

Tilden's first Wimbledon victory was achieved against Gerald Patterson in the challenge round which existed at that time. He lost the opening set 2–6, but reeled off the next three. The following year, he beat the South African, Brian Norton, this time dropping not only the first set but the second as well, before getting into his formidable stride.

In 1927 he seemed to have Cochet at his mercy, his power – abetted by tremendous skill – overwhelming the Frenchman's graceful game. Tilden won the first two sets, and was 5–2 up in the third. It seemed a formality, but it was not. Somehow Cochet rallied, and ran out with the match. One weird explanation was that Tilden had been hypnotized by Indian spectators! His third victory, against Wilmer Allison, was less dramatic, being achieved in straight sets.

Tilden deployed not only power but ferocious spin; so much so that the ball was sometimes distorted into the shape of an egg. There was no shot that he did not possess, and none that he had not studied. His book, *Match Play and the Spin of the Ball*, testified to the fact. His service was awesome in its speed, his back-hand an excellent shot – he had spent the winter of 1919 improving it, after he had lost that second American title to his friend and foe, Bill Johnston.

In the Davis Cup only two men ever managed to beat him in the singles, and both were French. Lacoste had the better of him twice, Cochet three times. Over all, Tilden's Davis Cup record was astounding. He won no fewer than thirty-four out of forty-one rubbers, twenty-one out of twenty-eight in the challenge round, with thirteen victories in twenty-two singles matches. His career lasted for ten successive years, by the end of which he was thirty-seven and far past his best; a fact which casts an even rosier light on the statistics. How would they have looked had he begun playing in his early twenties?

He took the United States singles title on seven occasions, winning finals in 1922 and 1925 against Bill Johnston which were among the finest and most dramatic in the story of the tournament. One of his most unusual matches was against the celebrated French woman champion, Suzanne Lenglen. Tilden was convinced that he could give her a start of forty points in every game and still win. When she refused, he gave them to her anyway by deliberately losing the first three points of each game. Despite that he was as good as his word, winning the opening set 6–o, and there was to be no other. Mlle Lenglen retired from the contest.

Retiring from amateur tennis, Tilden became a pioneer of the professional game, which was to lead an oddly hole-and-corner existence till its flowering in the 1970s. Tilden, making the most of his natural skills, his colossal experience, his flair for the dramatic and for occasional gamesmanship – though not the crude kind we have become so used to today – ornamented the pro tour till he was well into his fifties.

In 1945, having played many matches for charity during the war, Tilden suggested to a group of leading young professionals, such as Bobby Riggs and Don Budge, who were all then practising at the Los Angeles tennis club, that they stage a tournament for some deserving cause. Note that Tilden, from the east, had by now found his way to California, whose players would dominate American tennis for so many years, indeed until the emergence of Connors and McEnroe in the seventies. Out of his idea – which did not go down too well with players in need of money – grew not only a hard court tournament, but the Professional Players' Association, with Tilden as its tournament manager.

Despite the fact that he was by now fifty-two, Tilden had amazing success on the circuit. In the opening tournament, of which he was director, he actually won through to the semi-finals, after beating the hefty young Lester Stoefen 7–5 and a staggering 6–0 in the quarter-finals. Having gone down to Budge, he faced another far younger man in the brilliantly accomplished Fred Perry of England to contest third place. Tilden, who had actually come back from being 5–1 down in the first set to Stoefen, gave another fantastic performance, beating Perry in three sets.

He was still able to serve with power and accuracy, hit winners off his forehand, and if his backhand had now come down to a defensive chop, he was amazingly ready to go for winners, eschewing the easy shot.

Tilden, always a wily foe, was able to outfox even as fierce a competitor as Perry. 'I was a great believer,' said Perry in later years, 'if you get a man down, stamp on him.' But Tilden skilfully and shrewdly drew his sting by praising his splendid stroke play, telling him what a pleasure it was to play against him, lulling him into long rallies, then suddenly raising his own game, pouncing, and beating him. Even the highly competitive Bobby Riggs, 1939 winner of Wimbledon, found Tilden very hard to beat, and quite fascinating. 'Bill,' he wrote, 'had all the players hypnotized.'

Not to mention the crowds and occasionally the umpire. When Tilden lost a point he thought he should have won, he would go into a routine, beseeching the skies for pity, which might have wrung tears from a basilisk; but he did not curse, bully and insult umpires as too many of his present-day successors have done.

A frustrated actor, he could play on the feelings of spectators, as he did once at a tournament played in Pasadena at the Huntington Hotel. He was pitted against a very good player called Johnny Faunce in a most exciting, talented game. There was an umpire but no linesman. After a long rally, with Tilden running like a man less than half his age, Faunce hit a thundering drive down the line. Tilden did not try to play it. He simply caught the ball, looked at the umpire, and told him it was out. The umpire fell into line.

'How could you possibly call that ball out, Bill?' asked a furious but restrained Johnny Faunce, coming to the net. 'I'm calling them over here, John,' said Tilden, coolly; then he walked over to the crowd. 'Ladies and gentlemen,' he announced, 'we're playing a match for money, and we have to call them as we

see them.' Game, set and match, in every sense. The
crowd applauded him ecstatically, and a demoralized
Faunce lost the match. No wonder. When Tilden
asked the pro player Wayne Sabin why he thought he
had done so well against Riggs, Sabin replied, 'Hell,
Bill, you intimidated him, just as you do all the rest
of us.'

There was, alas, a darker side to Tilden, one which
intermittently got him into trouble with the law, and
saddened his later years. These were lonely and
wretched. He died in 1953, at the age of only sixty, but
his prowess and prestige on the tennis court have
splendidly survived him.

Tilden used to call Jean Borotra, his French opponent, 'goat-getter', which suggests that, from time to
time, the biter had been bit. Certainly Borotra,
who English newspapers nicknamed the Bounding
Basque, was as great or greater a showman as Tilden.
The man who once upstaged him was Fred Perry.
Perry knew Borotra had a habit of missing a shot, by
design or accident, careering on over the line, and
ending up among the crowd in the lap of a pretty girl,
thus delighting a crowd which would henceforth be
on his side. During a tournament in Paris, Perry and
Pat Hughes, another British player, went into town,
visited an *haute couture* boutique, and persuaded the
manageress to 'lend' them a mannequin for the afternoon. This, after some bewilderment, she did, so it
was Perry, not Borotra, who 'missed' his shot in the
first set and ended up in the embrace of a pretty girl!
Perry it was, in due course, who won the match.

I have referred to Three Musketeers, but really
there were four, since Brugnon was a valuable aide to
Borotra, Cochet and Lacoste. These three, however,

are the ones best remembered. In his inevitable beret,
Borotra always took the eye; he and Henri Cochet
were the spectacular members of the team, while
Lacoste's superb results were the fruit of patient
study. He was, if there ever has been, an intellectual
of the tennis court, a man whose game and whose success were a sustained triumph of mind over matter.

Borotra was taught tennis, he once explained to me,
by an Englishwoman, Mrs Wildy, 'my dear holidays'
mother'. He would come to England to stay in Kenley,
Surrey, learning English. He was in fact fourteen when
she asked him whether he would like to play tennis.
'Do you think you'll be able to hit the ball?' she said.
As a good Basque, Borotra replied, 'I've played pelota,
I can hit it with the hand. I think I can hit it with a
racket; it's much bigger.'

Indeed he could, to spectacular purpose. He would
win Wimbledon in 1924 and 1926, and play a major
part in France's six-year domination of the Davis Cup.
He went on playing competitive tennis, such as the
Queen's Cup between Britain and France, till comfortably into his sixties. Indeed, he played not only in
the fiftieth such contest, but in all forty-nine before.
His longevity he ascribed to a robust childhood, discipline, willpower and what he called 'physical
jerks'. No one in England seemed to hold his connec-
tion with the Vichy Government, as Minister of Sports,
against him; his allegiance to Pétain, the old marshal
who collaborated with the Nazis, survived well into
the 1970s, when he was among the leaders of those who
demanded that Pétain be given a new burial.

Borotra was another of those players of the twenties
– and even the thirties – who came from a solid
middle-class background. Unlike Bill Tilden, how-

ever, he never made tennis his whole life. He was a genuine amateur, a man with degrees in law and engineering, who became a highly successful businessman; as, indeed, did his fellow musketeer, Lacoste. His impressive list of championships, which included the French and Australian singles, would have been longer still had he not put his work first and avoided tournaments which would conflict with it. For all that, he played for sixteen successive years in the French Davis Cup team, and set up a record for the number of rubbers he had contested. He was known to return to Paris from Wimbledon between rounds for business conferences. At Wimbledon itself, he once held a business meeting in the bath just after beating his colleague Lacoste in the 1927 semi-final.

His beret and his long white trousers should not be allowed to conceal the fact that the essence of Borotra's game was his dynamism. Few have been better and more resilient on the volley. He had not the versatility and the repertory of strokes of a Tilden, perhaps not even of a Lacoste, but he made up for this with his furious fitness, and with his clever tactics. Before him, few had been subtle enough to realize that if you play too hard on an opponent's apparent weakness you may coax it to become a strength. Thus, in that 1927 semi-final against Lacoste, he felt he had identified a chink in his opponent's armour, but he probed it only for a couple of games in the earlier sets, returning to attack it ferociously in the fifth. He made his first appearance for the French Davis Cup team in 1922; his last, astonishingly, in 1947.

Henri Cochet was equally long-lived on the courts, continuing into his late sixties. Nicknamed the Little Man from Lyons, his style was tantalizingly different

from Borotra's. Where Borotra was perpetual motion
incarnate, Cochet could sometimes seem quite casual,
almost uninterested. If art, as the Romans had it, is
to conceal art, then Cochet was an artist indeed, for
his play had about it a kind of nonchalant brilliance.
With his exceptional eye, his sublime positional sense,
his talent for the half-volley, his mastery of the area
between the back line and the service line, his capacity
to hit the rising ball, and his instant reflexes, he had
the better even of Bill Tilden. Indeed, on the nine
occasions that they met, Cochet seven times ran out
the victor; including that extraordinary recovery at
Wimbledon. (Another, none too convincing, explanation given for Tilden's strange fall from grace was
that he was anxious to show off his service to the King.)

Born in 1901, Cochet took up tennis much earlier
than Borotra, at the age of seven. Between 1928 and
1931 he was widely regarded as the best player in the
world. He won Wimbledon twice, in 1927 and in 1929,
his victim in both finals being none other than Borotra. The second final was a straight sets affair, the first
was infinitely closer run. Just as with Tilden, he found
himself two sets down, but won the next two. In the
third set – another parallel with his match against
Tilden – he was 5–2 down in the final set. Six times
match point was against him, six times he saved it,
and he went on to win the title. He won the French
championship on five occasions, the American in 1928,
turned professional in 1933, but reverted to amateur
status after the Second World War. At the age of forty-
nine he was still good enough to win the British
Covered Courts doubles title with Jaroslav Drobny.

Jean René Lacoste was four years younger than Cochet. He had none of the exuberance of Borotra and
Cochet, being a taciturn man who carefully studied

his adversaries, setting down his analyses in notebooks. He favoured the back of the court, lobbed beautifully, and had a cast-iron backhand. He defeated both his fellow Musketeers, Borotra and Cochet, in Wimbledon finals (where Borotra also held a decision over him) and had a remarkable ascendancy over Bill Tilden – the product of planning.

When America beat France in the challenge round of the 1926 Davis Cup, Lacoste studied Tilden, to beat him. He lost the opening set 4–6, but came back splendidly to take the next three in a row, 6–4, 8–6, 8–6. No small feat for a player who had initially taken up tennis for his health, and who was never very strong. Two more famous victories over Tilden lay ahead; one the following year in the French singles final, the other that same year in the challenge round, ironically in Tilden's own Philadelphia.

Illness forced him to retire in 1929. He came back three years later to beat the Wimbledon champion, Sidney Woods, in the French championships, but was soon forced back into a sadly premature retirement. It is odd to think that he should produce in time so roundly robust a daughter as Catherine Lacoste, who became amateur women's golf champion of the United States.

Jacques Brugnon, rather older than the others, being born in 1895, excelled in doubles play. Partnering one or other of them, he won twenty-three out of the thirty-two doubles matches he played in the Davis Cup for France in the period from 1921 to 1932, and was seven times a doubles finalist at Wimbledon, winning four times, twice with Borotra and twice with Cochet.

In the meantime, there was also, and exotically, Suzanne Lenglen. No player did more to make women's tennis popular. When she reached her first Wimbledon final in 1919 to play the formidable Mrs Lambert Chambers, the intense interest among the spectators necessitated its being played on the Centre Court, where it was attended by the King and Queen.

There was about Mlle Lenglen's life, her play, her whole public persona, an undertow of vibrant pathos. It was often said that she moved like a dancer, but in many ways the analogy seemed rather with an actress. She had the presence, the imperious dignity, the aquiline looks. She had, if not a stage mother, then a tennis court father, who had drilled and driven her towards perfection from an early age, making her play endless shots at a handkerchief. She had a temperament which went beyond the merely Gallic and which led her at last to fall out even with the adoring Wimbledon crowd, committing the cardinal sin of all, that of Keeping the Royal Family Waiting, which would be repeated by the controversial Jimmy Connors half a century later.

Mrs Lambert Chambers stood up to her wonderfully well in that 1919 final. She had already made Lenglen's acquaintance in 1913 at Cannes, when the French girl was only thirteen. Mrs Lambert Chambers – originally Miss Dorothea Douglass – had won, but had been greatly impressed. She herself had a magnificent record at Wimbledon, where she had won the first of her seven titles as long ago as 1903. She was forty-one by the time she played Lenglen in the challenge round, and did so well that it is legitimate to wonder how Lenglen would have fared against her when she was in her prime.

She lost the first set only by 10–8 and still, though she was giving away twenty-one years, was spry enough to take the second set 6–4. She was 4–1 behind in the third set, but her morale and her physical condition were such that she overhauled Mlle Lenglen, reaching match point at 6–5. Only an outrageous piece of bad luck robbed her of success, for Mlle Lenglen flailed at a ball which seemed to have beaten her, connected with the edge of her racket, took the point and survived to win 9–7. To play a record number of forty-four games – one which would not be beaten for fifty-one years in the women's final – and still come so near at so late an age was an achievement indeed by Mrs Lambert Chambers.

Mlle Lenglen, however, proved to be unbeatable. In 1920 the doughty Mrs Lambert Chambers fought her way through to the challenge round, where Lenglen beat her 6–3, 6–0, besides winning the women's singles in the Olympic Games at Antwerp, which had lawn tennis among its sports. It should be said that when Mlle Lenglen played at Wimbledon in 1919, it was her first experience of grass courts, which made her success the more remarkable.

Altogether, she won Wimbledon six times between 1919 and 1925, the missing year being 1924 when ill-health forced her to withdraw. She was French champion half a dozen times as well, the first in 1920, the last in 1926. Doubtless she would have won Wimbledon yet again in 1926, but a dispute with the tournament's referee led her first to keep the Queen waiting for thirty minutes, then to her withdrawal. She never played there again, retiring to turn professional, and to run a successful coaching school in Paris.

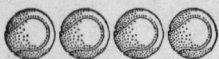

Little Miss Poker Face, Perry and Austin

1924, the year in which Lenglen missed Wimbledon,
saw the women's title go to an excellent English player,
Kitty McKane, who, brought up on badminton, was
consequently a strong and splendid volleyer. Her victim in the final was a nineteen-year-old American girl
called Helen Wills, who would, after Lenglen's retirement, proceed to dominate the women's game.

A doctor's daughter from sunny Berkeley, in California, she was always admired rather than liked; the
nickname, Little Miss Poker Face, tells us much about
the way she was regarded. Significantly, her chief rival
during her long years of dominance was another Californian from Berkeley, Helen Jacobs. The 'sunshine
state' was turning out players as if by conveyor belt.
In retrospect it is extraordinary that France and Britain should remain so long in contention at the highest
levels, for the natural advantages of the Californian
and Australian climate were bound to tell in the end.
Since the days of the Four Musketeers, French tennis
has languished. Even when the Wimbledon title did
go back to France in 1946, won by the towering Yvon
Petra, it was largely because Jack Kramer had injured
his hand.

But sunshine alone could scarcely account for the
long pre-eminence of Californians and Australians.
Young people from young nations, they had also – not

least in the person of Little Miss Poker Face – a sharply
competitive attitude to the game. It has been given the
ugly name 'killer instinct'. Perry, as we have seen,
manifested it, but in later years neither the English
nor the French seemed able to produce such players;
those whose temperament matched their talent. When
Bjorn Borg emerged in the 1970s, he was another
'freak', a marvellous player from a country, Sweden,
which had not thrown one up for years.

Sweden, with its rigorously limited months of sunshine, would seem on the face of it to have none of
the characteristics to nurture tennis champions. But
then, by the same token, neither has Czechoslovakia,
which gave the game the popular and resilient Jaroslav Drobny in the 1940s and 1950s, and Navratilova
and the rest in our own time.

Helen Wills, who would become Wills Moody when
she married, was not very quick on the court, but her
ground strokes were extremely powerful and she bit-
terly contested every point. To be beaten was purga-
tory to her. In the 1933 American singles final at
Forest Hills, Helen Jacobs was for once getting the
better of her, winning 8–6, 3–6, 3–0 and well on the
way to victory, when Mrs Moody developed a myster-
ious injury to her leg and retired. More mysteriously
still, it had healed sufficiently, she said, for her to contest the women's doubles final later in the afternoon,
but she was eventually persuaded that it was better
not to play.

Helen Wills had her defenders, too, those who insisted that her reputation did her less than justice,
that it was acquired largely because, unlike most
players on the tennis circuit, she was able to talk about
other things. She could paint and write, as well as

play tennis. Such rounded figures are rare today as most players have to apply themselves single-mindedly to the game to achieve any measure of success against the fierce competition.

Only once did Helen Wills play Suzanne Lenglen, and that was in a little-remembered match at Cannes in the south of France in 1926; one which caused a furore of interest at the time. A grandstand was fashioned by taking off the roof tiles of one of the villas which overlooked the court. When a call of 'Out!' suggested that Mlle Lenglen had won the match, spectators invaded the court to congratulate her, only for a brave British line judge, Lord Charles Hope, to push a way through them and declare that the ball had not been out at all; the cry had come from a spectator. So the game was resumed, and Lenglen still won it. Her father, who never missed a game she played, had determined before she was twelve years old that she would become 'the most absolute mistress of every stroke and every branch of lawn tennis'. A Svengali indeed. It was said that when M. Lenglen was absent, his daughter looked shaky and vulnerable. Poor thing. When she died in July 1938, she was still but thirty-nine years old.

Helen Wills Moody was more compact and resilient. In 1922, at sixteen, she reached all three finals of the United States championships, losing the singles to Mrs Molla Mallory, who the previous year had defeated Lenglen in the tournament. Illness caused Lenglen to retire after the first set. But Helen Wills won the first of her seven American titles the following year, and went on winning them till 1931. Her record at Wimbledon was even more extraordinary. She took the women's singles title eight times, the first in 1927,

the last eleven years later, remaining unbeaten in all
singles matches between 1927 and 1932. If she was not
quick, her fine sense of anticipation largely made up
for that.

Four times she met and beat Helen Hull Jacobs in
the Wimbledon final. Four times she won, though in
1935 Miss Jacobs had match point at 5–3 and threw
it away with a careless shot. In 1938 it was Miss Jacobs,
a fine volleyer with a strong backhand, who hurt an
already injured ankle, limping through what became
a mere procession. Unlike Helen Wills Moody, five
years earlier at Forest Hills, however, she bravely decided that the show must go on.

Britain, having invented the game and inevitably
dominated it in its early years, had been wholly over-
shadowed by the French, the Americans and the Australians since the First World War. In 1933, however,
they began an extraordinary four-year dominance of
the Davis Cup, which can be seen in retrospect as
Britain's swan song. Never again have players of the
calibre of Perry, Austin and company emerged to
conquer the world. It is at once pleasant and a little
sad to look back on that short, halcyon time.

As the Davis Cup increased and multiplied, changes
had been made, though the controversial challenge
round remained. Zoning was inaugurated in 1923 to
cut down the amount of travelling, mainly by sea at
that time. There were four entries in the first American zone, a dozen in the European. In 1952 an
Eastern zone was begun. Since countries were able to
challenge where they chose, this geographical nomen-
clature could often be confusing. South Africa, until
it was expelled, usually competed in the European

zone. Brazil alternated between the European and the American zones.

It is an intriguing coincidence that both Fred Perry and Ann Haydon Jones, one of Britain's very few postwar Wimbledon singles champions, should have begun as table tennis players. On the face of it, one game is no real preparation for the other, even if table tennis clearly promotes footwork, fitness and general alertness.

Perry was born in Stockport, Cheshire, in 1909, the son of a Labour Member of Parliament. He was a superb table tennis player, winning the world title in 1928 and 1929. He was persuaded to take up lawn tennis by members of the Herga Club, in Harrow, and his greatest asset was, from the first, his 'running forehand'. His backhand, by contrast, was, in the words of one famous opponent, 'almost entirely a defensive shot'. With short balls, however, he could take a heavy, slicing, backhand shot, then rush to the net for the return. As for his service, it was adequate rather than ferocious, the oddest thing about it being that his second service was an almost exact, if somewhat slower and more cautious, replica of his first. Where the majority of leading players would put all the speed they could behind their first service, then slice and spin the second, Perry would scarcely change his.

His forehand, employed on the rising ball, was probably the finest of his time, and he could take it as he dashed towards the net. Lesser men had to set themselves to strike the ball. Not Perry. Risks were implicit in his forehand style, but he was glad to live with them. Moreover, he did not vary his grip. His wrists, however, were immensely strong, perhaps the product of table tennis, and this enabled him to flick the ball. Fast, elegant, an admirable volleyer with an unusual sense of anticipation, he was certainly the best English player between the wars, and probably the finest of all time.

His adventurous style took a while to be properly developed and refined, but once it was there was no stopping him. In 1929 he won through the Wimbledon qualifying tournament, got to the third round of the competition proper, and there lost to John Olliff. The following year he gave up table tennis, though in 1932 he was still good enough to beat a leading French player in Paris.

It was in 1930, in the British Hard Courts championship – traditionally held at Bournemouth till the commercialism of pro tennis effectively killed it in the late 1970s – that Perry established himself. He played Bunny Austin, then the acknowledged star of British tennis, held match point against him and only narrowly went down. The two of them would be the backbone and inspiration of the future British Davis Cup team, complementing one another perfectly.

Where Perry was extrovert, competitive, athletic, even brash, Austin was gentle, almost fragile, prevailing through the sheer excellence of his technique and skills.

1931 saw Perry reach the semi-finals both at Wimbledon and Forest Hills, and play for Britain against France in the challenge round of the Davis Cup. He defeated Borotra, but lost the only singles he ever did lose in the Davis Cup – a thrilling four-set match against Henri Cochet which decided the issue. Perry won all his nine other individual rubbers in the Davis Cup; his overall record in the competition was forty-five wins in fifty-two rubbers.

In 1933 Perry won the first of his three American

singles titles; in 1934 he began his extraordinary sequence at Wimbledon of three consecutive titles: a record to be equalled only four decades later by Bjorn Borg who would be congratulated on court by Perry himself. Borg broke the record the following year, but it was a magnificent one.

1934 was Perry's great year. He beat the Wimbledon champion, Jack Crawford of Australia, in the Australian final, then defeated him again in straight sets at Wimbledon itself. At Forest Hills he won the American title with a five-set win over Wilmer Allison in the final. In 1935 and 1936 his victim in the Wimbledon final was the stylish, sporting and aristocratic German, Gottfried von Cramm, whom he beat each time in straight sets. The second of his successes was by way of being a revenge, for von Cramm had had the temerity to beat him in the final of the French championships. 'He'll have a lot of trouble stretching to the right,' a friendly Wimbledon masseur told Perry, who proceeded to thrash the German 6–1, 6–1, 6–0. The Nazis were not a bit pleased, and later put poor von Cramm in prison for a misdemeanour which would surely have been overlooked had he won. Perry followed this triumph with another success in the American championships, defeating the renowned Donald Budge in the final.

Meanwhile, in the Davis Cup, he, Austin and the rest were carrying all before them. In the 1933 challenge round they beat the French 3–2 in Paris; in 1934 they beat America 4–1 at Wimbledon; in 1935 they improved that to a 5–0 whitewash; while in 1936 they beat the Australians 3–2, Perry defeating Crawford in the decisive singles. In 1936 he turned professional, being by then very much the darling of the

Hollywood stars, who had taken to tennis with immense enthusiasm.

It was said of Perry that he kept his own private score of each game in his head, awarding himself points he felt ought to have been his, so that there was, so to speak, a text beneath the text. He had almost total recall of the matches and the shots he had played, astonishing opponents by the vividness with which he remembered them. 'He is possibly,' wrote Bobby Riggs, 'the most tireless replay fiend in tennis.' Once, playing Riggs on the court, he showed the extent of his competitive urge by pointing to a ball left on court and remarking dryly, 'You might step on it, and that would be a pity.'

His professional career lasted well into his forties, and was marked by an intense rivalry with Donald Budge, whom he would refer to as J. Donald God. He loved to beat him. Budge, the first player ever to achieve the so-called Grand Slam when he won the Australian, Wimbledon, Forest Hills and French championships of 1938, was red-haired, 6 feet 3 inches tall and famous for the power of his 'rolled' backhand. If Perry thought him conceited, others pronounced him 'modest and good-natured'. Certainly he was his own man, the one player on the post-war professional tour notably immune to the blandishments and stratagems of Bill Tilden.

Bunny Austin was a player almost designed for the Davis Cup, as its duration, shorter than any tournament, did not tax his vulnerable physique.

Henry Wilfred Austin came from a tennis-playing family in the suburban comfort of Norwood. His father encouraged both him and his sister Joan – later a good tournament player as Mrs Lycett – and on wet

afternoons they would bang the ball against the nur-
sery wall. At Repton, where he was also an excellent
cricketer, he became Public Schools champion at
Queen's Club in 1921, and Junior champion of the
United Kingdom at Weybridge the following year.
Then he went to Cambridge where, inevitably, he
was a tennis Blue, aspiring in the meanwhile to far
higher things in British tournaments. His ground
strokes were beautifully made, but they had to compensate for indifferent smashing and an undistin-
guished service. Artistry, in a word, made up for a
want of physique.

Until Perry came along, Austin was clearly the best
British player to emerge since the war, and probably
the best since the days of the Dohertys. Certainly he
was the first Englishman to reach the Wimbledon
final for a decade when, in 1932, he met the powerful
American, Ellsworth Vines. Of lesser importance was
the fact that he was the first man to wear tennis shorts
at Wimbledon. Perry, at times, used to wear them
too, though he hated them. When the two of them got
together in the Davis Cup team, they were, as we have
seen, almost invincible.

Alas for Austin, he found Vines, that day at Wimbledon, in the finest form of his mercurial career. If
Austin was one of the most fragile champions of his
time, then Vines was one of the most powerful. His
service, when it was really functioning, was quite awesome; the ace with which he concluded his one-sided
match with Austin was long remembered for its speed
and force. Only twenty-one years old at the time,
which made him five years younger than Austin, he
won in straight sets 6–4, 6–2, 6–0, having done the
same to Jack Crawford of Australia in the semi-final.

In the last three rounds of Wimbledon his overhead play and service in general were ferociously good. There was no way Austin, for all his high technique, could live with him in such form.

But Vines never could sustain such form. The following year he again got to the final, where he met his 1932 victim, Crawford. This time, however, much of the virtue seemed to have gone out of him and he lost in five sets. Some months later he turned professional and Wimbledon never saw him again.

His was a tantalizing career. Slender, 6 feet 5 inches tall, a natural athlete who would later – a familiar story – become a fine golfer, Vines as an amateur left scarcely any margin for error. A shot was either irresistibly good, or horribly bad. How sad that professionalism should debar him from the world game at large, for in playing Tilden, Perry and their like, he became a far better performer. Change of pace, topspin, sustained rallying and the capacity to relax now gave variety and sophistication to his play, though it was too late for Wimbledon ever to see it. As for his service, many opponents thought it the best ever seen. There was a superbly integrated rhythm to Vines's service action, he volleyed splendidly, his forehand was described by a contemporary as 'possibly the most devastating shot ever developed in tennis'. When Donald Budge, who beat Austin in the 1938 Wimbledon final, turned professional and toured with Vines in 1939, he came out ahead only by a margin of twenty-two to seventeen matches, in the course of which Vines had an average of two service aces per game against him.

In 1938 Austin was ranked second in the world, as indeed he had been in 1931. Sidney Wood, who won

Wimbledon that year, was indirectly the cause of
Austin's defeat seven years later. He it was who coaxed
Budge to forsake his cautious, baseline play and develop into a glorious all-court player. Budge's story,
indeed, is a curious one of handicaps and reluctance
overcome. The son of a Scottish professional footballer
who had settled in California, he much preferred a
variety of sports, among them football, cycling and
roller skating, to tennis. At the age of fifteen, however,
his family persuaded him to enter the California
championships. These he won, though it was the first
tournament in which he had ever played. From that
moment tennis was his sport, though it would be
several years before he lost his intense shyness.

In 1933 he had something of a rehearsal for his
Wimbledon final five years later, beating Austin in
the quarter-finals. In 1938 he became the first player
to win the title without dropping a set since the challenge round was abolished. One of the most unusual
features of his distinguished career was that, just as
some golfers have radically altered their swing, so
Budge, at the comparatively late age of twenty, re-
modelled his forehand. He went back from the east of
the United States to Oakland, California, and worked
under a celebrated coach, Tom Stowe, till he had
utterly changed his forehand action. It would never
be his best stroke but it was radically improved.

He was formidable at the net, served strongly, and
had a phenomenally precise backhand, but could
never quite overcome a tendency to keep his forehand
too low, perhaps because the stroke was not natural
to him. Power was the essence of his game; he called
clay-court tennis 'girls' tennis'. But a wily player like
little Bobby Riggs, the shrewd Californian who won

Wimbledon in 1939, was a match for him on subsequent professional tours.

As for Austin, he won no fewer than thirty-six of the forty-eight singles he played in the Davis Cup for Great Britain between 1929 and 1937, beating Vines and Budge themselves in the course of his career, not to mention Jack Crawford. Later, he would be drawn into the toils of the Moral Rearmament movement, emigrating to the United States where, in 1943, he asked for exemption from his call-up for military service. His father, it was announced, was 'disappointed in his son'. There was a spiteful campaign against him in the British press, and the tennis establishment never forgave him.

Austin did in fact join the American army during the war, but trouble with his heart and liver prevented him from becoming an officer and going overseas. When one thinks of all the able-bodied professional footballers who spent the war comfortably in Aldershot because they were drafted into the physical education corps, one marvels at the fuss that was made about poor Austin.

When he returned to England, it was to be told that his membership of the All England Lawn Tennis Club had lapsed. The decent and generous thing would have been simply to reinstate him. Not a bit of it. He was placed on the waiting list, where he remained for nearly twenty years, the Club huffing and puffing that he had been sent three reminders to pay his subscription while in the States. 'There were a large number of candidates on the waiting list,' the club secretary explained, 'with very good claims to membership, and it was not felt that he could be given priority.'

One wonders who could possibly have a better claim to membership than Bunny Austin, with the sole and possible exception of Fred Perry. Austin himself felt that hostility among certain members to Moral Rearmament was behind the snub, as it may well have been. Yet however much, and with whatever justification, one may dislike that movement, it is no excuse for maltreating a gentle, decent, honourable man, who happens besides to be one of the finest players Britain has ever produced.

As it is, Fred Perry and other old friends take Austin into the members' tent at Wimbledon. 'I don't suppose many soldiers did [pay their subscriptions],' Austin has said. 'I can't imagine a man fighting at El Alamein saying, "Hang on a minute, Jerry, I just want to post off my All England sub." '

Austin admits, 'I still don't know which side the ball passed me,' when Vines beat him with that last ace in the Wimbledon final of 1932. 'All I can remember is the thud of the backstopping behind me. I didn't play well that day, but, by Jove, Ellie did. He served thirty aces in twelve games. Six years later in my other Wimbledon final I did much better, but Donald Budge was so good that day he was unplayable. He devoured all my best shots. He was truly magnificent.'

Even as a young Reptonian, Austin was reported by his housemaster as 'a small and delicate child' who had periodically to be sent to bed 'for a few days' rest'. This was despite his tennis and his splendid record as an opening bat. By contrast Perry, intent on physical fitness, trained regularly with the players of the Arsenal football club, who then dominated the English game. He was no mean footballer himself.

If he loathed shorts, then Austin, when he wore them first in 1932, actually had them designed by his tailor, not at all on the current brief lines, but after the fashion of the rugby field!

The 1939 women's champion was yet another Californian, Alice Marble, who had a raking stride and who had bravely overcome, five years earlier, anaemia and pleurisy which were wrongly diagnosed as tuberculosis.

During those largely barren years for British women, the flag was flown by the talented Dorothy Round, winner of the singles in 1934, when she took advantage of the absence of Helen Wills to beat Helen Jacobs in the final, and in 1937, when she defeated the Polish girl, Jedrzejowska, in a gruelling three sets. A Methodist who would not play on Sundays and thus had problems in Continental tournaments, Dorothy Round at her best was a delight to watch, both strong and precise. Diligent practice and polishing of her strokes led her even to be compared with Suzanne Lenglen.

Jack Kramer, the Pros and the Australians

The war over, and Wimbledon flourishing again, there was no doubt who was the dominant player in the world: another Californian, Jack Kramer. Even before the war began, he had established himself as a player of immense potential. Tall and strong, eager to go to the net where his forehand volley was almost impossible to return and his backhand volley not much less effective, he established a record when, at the age of eighteen years and two weeks, he played for the United States in the challenge round against Australia as doubles partner to Joe Hunt; one day after Britain declared war on Nazi Germany.

It was awfully hard to find a weakness in Kramer's splendid game. His first service was lethal enough with its tendency to swing an opponent out to the right, and it was varied in turn by one of sheer, devastating power. His second service, however, was also capable of scoring aces, with its so-called American twist, heavily sliced so that it hopped high and hit with unusual force. Alternatively, Kramer could hit his second service hard and fast to the other side. On the forehand, however, he avoided stratagems, simply relying on his pace.

Perhaps the fact that he developed blisters on his racket hand, thereby causing him to lose to the popular and ebullient Czech, Jaroslav Drobny, at Wimble-

don in 1946, was due in some measure to his grip; an
Eastern grip, in which he held the racket very high,
the butt of it in his hand.

When he smashed, Kramer rarely made a mistake.
In this aspect of his game he perhaps had less force
than his contemporary, Ted Schroeder, but he had
infinitely more precision, and he was incomparably
better on the ground.

What he did not have, at least in the earlier years
of a remarkable career, was luck. Not only did he lose
the 1946 Wimbledon but he also went down bizarrely
in the American nationals of 1942 and 1943. In 1942
he was the hot favourite, but just as he was about to
leave California for Forest Hills, appendicitis struck.

In 1943, by now a coastguard training in Connecti-
cut, Kramer did reach the final. He was the strong
favourite again, but ate clams the previous day, was
severely sick, and lost to Joe Hunt. In 1946, however,
he took the title, and in 1947 nothing and nobody
could stop him winning Wimbledon, beating his
compatriot Tom Brown in straight sets in the final.
It was also the year in which he and Ted Schroeder
recaptured the Davis Cup for the United States, with
a victory over the Australians in Melbourne.

To his physical assets and variety of strokes he had
added a very shrewd approach which he called playing
the percentages; a new kind of strategy whereby each
shot was judged to give him the greatest and his opponent the least advantage.

Having abundantly proved his point at Melbourne,
Wimbledon and Forest Hills, Kramer turned professional, entering what one might call that distinguished, twilight world in which the prestige could
never match the prizes. His first match was played

on 26 December 1947 against the ebullient Bobby Riggs, gambler, rebel and competitor extraordinary, in Madison Square Garden. No transport could make its way through fifteen inches of snow, but the subway was working, and over 15,000 fans saw the match won by Riggs, who had won ten out of eleven matches against Kramer when he was a young amateur. As a professional, however, he was scarcely in the same class, Kramer ending their protracted series 69–20 ahead.

When the gifted young Mexican-American, Pancho Gonzales, turned pro very early in his career, Kramer overwhelmed him, too, 96–27. Pancho Segura, the double-handed little player from Ecuador, won twenty-eight times against Kramer but lost sixty-four, while Frank Sedgman, the blond, tall Australian, came much closer, winning forty-one times, but losing fifty-four. Player turned promoter, with colossal skill and success. Kramer made $128,000 out of his tour with Sedgman. That may seem like chicken feed today, but taking inflation into account, it was then a great deal of money.

As the grand old man of professionalism, Kramer walked a tightrope between the establishment and the commercial tennis world which the establishment mistrusted and resented, even though it was much more honest than their own hypocritical kind. Submerged professionalism in tennis had been rife well before the war, with heavy 'expenses' often paid under the counter, making it possible for a leading player to live well off the game. But whereas the Olympics would stagger on into the eighties, a morass of double-think and shamateurism, the pressures on tennis were simply too great, even though it would be 1967 before Kramer was able to put a professional tournament on the Centre Court at Wimbledon.

Patient, shrewd and persuasive, exploiting the fact that for some reason establishment figures had always seen him as a blue-eyed boy, at heart an amateur even when he turned pro, Kramer made steady progress. He banded the pros into an association and set up an international Grand Prix of competitions.

Back trouble and arthritis eventually forced Kramer out of the active professional game, yet even at the age of thirty-six he was good enough at Wembley Pool to beat the mighty young Australian Lew Hoad, who had just turned professional. When, in 1968, the International Lawn Tennis Federation at last put an end to subterfuge and rank dishonesty by saying yes to open tennis between pros and amateurs, Kramer was no longer in the driver's seat, but it is hardly conceivable that the pros and good sense would have won their battle without him.

There was further trouble to come. Five years later, by now no longer a promoter, but a well-known commentator and the executive director of the Association of Tennis Professionals, Kramer led his men's withdrawal from the Wimbledon championships of 1973. The reason was the decision of the Yugoslav Tennis Federation to ban their player Nikki Pilic for refusing to take part in a Davis Cup tie. For some years past, the status of that competition had been severely diminished by its refusal to include professionals. Gross distortion resulted, but now that professionals were recognized, they did not always want to put country before cash. Pilic's suspension, though reduced to a month by the I.L.T.F., would have included Wimbledon, so the A.T.P., which had been formed only the previous September, pulled out its more than seventy members in protest. Thus a diminished Wimbledon was won by the competent though hardly brilliant Czech, Jan Kodes.

Pancho Gonzales would remark in later years that Kramer 'got the better of me when I joined the pros, and I never had a chance to get back at him'. To see Gonzales as a handsome, dignified, grey-haired, quietly composed 52-year-old, it was hard to think of him as the aggressive, explosive prodigy he had been in his early days.

The son of a furniture finisher and set painter in Hollywood, Gonzales in 1943, aged fifteen, was already the best junior in southern California, with the height, the power, the pace and the touch to make him an outstanding prospect. Alas, he did not like to go to school, and his record of truancy brought him into conflict with Perry T. Jones, the arbiter of tennis in California. He was suspended from tournament play for two years. You can hardly wonder that his attitude to authority should thereafter be one of scepticism and resentment. 'A little arguing and fighting,' he has said, 'is a natural part of the game.'

In October 1945 Gonzales went into the Navy, to emerge a more mature but still a controversial figure. His skill had not been blunted. In 1948, his second year of tournament tennis, still only twenty years old, he confounded those who had given him little chance of the U.S. championship by winning at Forest Hills.

He blasted out the celebrated Frankie Parker in the quarter-finals, losing only the second set, dropped the first set to Jaroslav Drobny in the semi-final but won the next three, and beat South Africa's Eric Sturgess

in the final in straight sets, though the last one went to
twenty-six games.

The following year he did it again, beating Ted
Schroeder in the final, showing wonderful resilience.
He dropped the first set 16–18, the second 2–6, and
seemed down and out. Instead he reeled off the next
three for the loss of seven games. He had already won
the Wimbledon doubles, and since he now turned
professional Wimbledon did not see him again till
1969.

It was then that he won an astonishing match
against the 25-year-old American Charlie Pasarell, to
whom he was giving sixteen years. The match lasted
five hours, and ran overnight. When Gonzales ap-
pealed against the light, the Wimbledon crowd booed
him, but they were cheering him the following day
when he rallied to come from two sets behind, the
first stretching to a gargantuan forty-six games. When
he dropped the second set 1–6 all seemed over, but
back he came, just as he had done against Schroeder,
to win the third set 16–14, the fourth 6–3, the last
11–9. Gonzales's courage and willpower have always
been extraordinary; they were even to be seen as he
came from behind in the Albert Hall tournament for
veterans in late 1979, though one had heard him com-
plaining that he and other 'old birds' were at a hope-
less disadvantage.

One remembers, too, his dry aside that evening to a
ball boy. When knocking up before a game, he hit a
ball high into the rafters, where it stuck. Later, he
asked the boy, who was clearly not alert, 'Can I have
another ball? I need two; I only have one. I know I
lost one. I'm sorry.'

He had long been resident professional at Caesar's

Palace Hotel in the gambling city of Las Vegas. Six feet three inches tall, he had put on very little weight over the years; years in which he had been capable of surprising the likes of Trabert, the powerful American, Laver and Newcombe among the pros. 'Laver thought I was at my peak [at forty-two in 1970],' he remarked, 'but I've got news for you; I was at my peak at twenty-five.'

Surprisingly, he made a shaky beginning in the pros, but class inevitably told. He placed considerable emphasis on size and power, both of which he had – like Kramer and his hero, Budge – but in his later years, delicacy of shot and clever strategy made up for waning strength and speed.

About Wimbledon, he had understandable and justifiable reservations. Wimbledon umpires do browbeat the crowds and the crowds often behave abominably, even in that citadel of the bourgeoisie. 'At Wimbledon,' said Gonzales, 'they think the only way is the heavy-handed way, the strong-armed way.' For him, 'English linesmen and umpires are the worst I have ever seen, because they can't be wrong.' It was an opinion shared by Nastase, with whom Gonzales, predictably, has sympathized.

The early post-war years were not good years for British tennis, though the burden of Davis Cup play was sturdily carried by Tony Mottram and his foil, the patient, bespectacled Geoff Paish.

As a nineteen-year-old, Mottram reached the third round of the Wimbledon singles in 1939. Who knows how good he might have been had he not spent the ensuing six years rather more demandingly, as an R.A.F. pilot, for which he was awarded the Distinguished Flying Cross. Given that long gap, his career was remarkably impressive. He played fifty-six Davis Cup rubbers for Britain, he got to the Wimbledon doubles final of 1947 with the Australian Bill Sidwell, his backhand was one of the best of his day, and he could even use it to smash. He was a far more dedicated player than most of his British contemporaries, and it was appropriate that he should eventually become the national coach in 1970.

Everything about Mottram seemed perfectly of a piece: his sportsmanship, his war record, his good temper, and the pretty, blonde, tennis-playing Joy Gannon, whom he married. The more surprising, then, that the tennis-playing son they produced, Buster Mottram, should be so controversial a figure. Very large, talented but wholly lacking in his father's restraint and consistency, Mottram was one of the several English men players who, in the years following his father, flattered to deceive, but had their moments.

Buster's moment was probably the Davis Cup semifinal at Crystal Palace in 1978, when he and other members of the British team surpassed themselves by beating Australia and reaching the final against the United States. There, alas, illusions faded, but the achievement was a memorable one. To have Buster, with his partner Ilie Nastase, goading the umpire and holding up play in the Braniff Doubles tournament at Earls Court rather more than a year later, however, made one realize again what a change there has been in Anglo-Saxon attitudes. His sister, Linda, is herself an accomplished player.

Americans and Aussies

British women players had a hard time against the
Americans in the forties and fifties. Not till the
emergence of Christine Truman, Angela Mortimer
and Ann Haydon Jones did the balance begin at last
to tip, two of those girls winning the Wimbledon final,
one of them coming to the brink. The Wightman
Cup, inaugurated in 1923 by a celebrated player,
Mrs Wightman, yielded four British victories against
the American girls in the first eight meetings, but between 1931 and 1958 Britain could not win at all. The
pattern has been to play five singles and two doubles
matches. Mrs Wightman herself successfully took part
in the first meeting in the doubles, America achieving
a clean sweep of 7–0.

Betz, Hart, Brough and Dupont (*née* Osborne)
dominated women's tennis in the years following the
war. Pauline Betz, who as a child in California had
helped and encouraged the 1950 Wimbledon champion, Budge Patty, enabling him to be coached, was
the first post-war winner there herself, in 1946. Still
another fine table tennis player, her career was eaten
away by the war; she was twenty-seven by the time
she took Wimbledon, and stayed loyal to a baseline
game at a time when the serve–volley combination was
growing paramount, even among women players. She
was very mobile, highly alert, and had an exceptional
backhand. In 1947 she turned professional after a

brush – there were so many – with the American tennis establishment, making a reputation at bridge as
well as at lawn tennis.

Her victim in the 1946 final was the rangy Louise
Brough, still another Californian, who won the title
two years later, kept it two years more, and recaptured
it in 1955. Miss Brough, a shy woman who took up
tennis as a Los Angeles child in the hope of making
friends, played her first tournament in midwinter because a friend's mother put her name down. She had
a fine eye and a flair for spin and volleying. Dick
Skeen, a well-known Californian coach, took her in
hand. At her best – before trouble with her service
throw-up and tennis elbow undermined her game –
she played like a man: a Californian man. Yet when
the need arose, she could vary her play with great
skill, as she did in the Wimbledon final of 1955 against
Beverley Fleitz. Facing a player who used double-
fisted shots on either side and therefore had no backhand to attack, Miss Brough forsook the net in favour
of a strategy of spin and cunning angles. In all, she
won thirty-three major titles.

Sturdy Margaret Osborne won the title in 1947,
beating Doris Hart, who lost again the following year
to Louise Brough, but Miss Hart eventually won in
1951. Miss Osborne came from Oregon, not from
California, but she used the style of the Californian
Alice Marble as the model for her fast serving, hard
volleying, stylish game. At her best in doubles, she
took the Wimbledon doubles title no fewer than five
times and in 1962, at the age of forty-four, was still
good enough to record yet another victory in the
mixed doubles.

Doris Hart's career was a triumph of the will. An
injury to her right knee cap, while learning to walk,

crippled her for some time, and never allowed her to move with complete ease. At nine, by which time the family had moved from St Louis to the sunshine of Florida, she had a hernia, but when the surgeon said she should take exercise, she began, at ten, to play tennis with her brother, Bud. A local coach, Slim Herbert, saw her, and invited her to play on the courts of the opulent Roney Plaza Hotel, Miami Beach. She was away. At fifteen, in 1941, she was good enough to beat Pauline Betz, though in future years Betz would have the edge on her.

Her style was exceptional, whether it was in her service or her ground strokes; she transcended her ill luck (a speck of Australian sand in her eye meant an operation in 1949) to become the best woman player in the game. She won the mixed doubles at Wimbledon and Forest Hills five years in a row, and provided a glorious Wimbledon final against Little Mo Connolly in 1953, when she gallantly lost 6–8, 5–7.

The American men, meanwhile, continued to be formidable. It is remarkable how many of them emerged to win major titles. Thus, in 1948, it was Bob Falkenburg who won the Wimbledon final against the accomplished Australian veteran, John Bromwich. The following year the mighty Ted Schroeder did the trick, beating Jaroslav Drobny, the Czech. Drobny had left his own country, married an English woman player, taken Egyptian nationality, and become the toast of Wimbledon. A robust, bespectacled left-hander who had also been a fine ice hockey player, 'Drob' lost again to Australia's Frank Sedgman in the 1952 final, but two years later delighted Wimbledon by beating little Ken Rosewall – surely the best player never to win Wimbledon – in the final.

The sheer depth and variety of American talent at

this time was shown by two more players who took the
Wimbledon title: the tall, elegant Budge Patty won
in 1950, having put himself on a harder training
regimen, and the large, solid Dick Savitt won in
1951. Patty did very well to beat the accomplished
Sedgman, who dropped the first set 1–6 and (as Drobny
forecast to a journalist sitting near him in the stand)
found the handicap too much to retrieve. Patty's interesting philosophy was that different points in a
game were of differing value; some were worth fighting harder for than others. There was some correspon-
dence with the belief of his predecessor, Falkenburg,
whose maxim was, 'When you break through service,
press three times as hard.'

After Sedgman had terminated the American run
of five Wimbledon titles in a row, Vic Seixas resumed
it in 1953. Seixas came from Philadelphia, had started
tennis at the age of five, had flown as a test pilot in
New Guinea and preferred grass courts for their
speed. He was a great man for cutting, slicing and
topspinning; indeed, there were times when he
was the victim of his own somewhat exaggerated
strokes.

He played in his first tournament when he was
only ten, and beat an adult, who promptly gave up
the game for years. A good-looking, easy-going man
who was actually known to smile on court, Seixas
backed up his spin with a forceful service. No one
had heard of him when he arrived in 1950, but he
gave Drobny a three-hour game, one set going to 17–
15, and he won his own title in straight sets against
the stalwart Dane, Nielsen.

Next, it was Drobny's turn, but in 1955 the title
went, as it had long seemed likely to do, to the forceful Tony Trabert, heir-apparent to Jack Kramer, and

who later became Kramer's lieutenant in the professional game. Blond, close cropped and freckled, Trabert, who came to Wimbledon in 1950 at the age of nineteen, was the all-American boy. Like Seixas, he was not a Californian. He came from Cincinnati. He was still a college student in 1950 when Tony Mottram, on one of his really good days, thrashed him 6–1, 6–4, 6–1 in the second round; but he, like General MacArthur, would be back.

It took him five years, and again the runner-up was the brave but unlucky Kurt Nielsen. Trabert beat him in straight sets, and indeed did not drop one throughout the tournament. The protégé of another Cincinnati man, the elegant Bill Talbert, Trabert at first wanted to use his strong physique to become a football player. Injuries to his older brother turned him to tennis instead. He hit the ball extremely hard, especially on the backhand, and had an inflexible sense of purpose.

The previous year he had played, with Seixas, a great part in wresting the Davis Cup from Australia, beating the rising Lew Hoad – a player whose power matched his own – in the singles and joining with Seixas to beat Hoad and Rosewall in the decisive doubles. Australia, however, guarded and cherished that cup as though it were their own, and the following year the Americans were whitewashed. Trabert, with two American and two French championships also behind him, promptly turned professional.

Between 1950 and 1967 Australia only three times failed to win the challenge round of the Davis Cup, each time being beaten by the United States. Three times they won the trophy four years in a row (1950–53, 1959–62 and 1964–7), and once they won it three years in a row (1955–7). Whatever happened at Wimbledon and Forest Hills, the inspired, demanding managership of Harry Hopman saw to it that the cup stayed almost unvaringly down under.

Hopman himself was a very competent singles player and strategist, an excellent doubles player, who with his brisk and likeable wife, originally Nell Hall, lost the mixed doubles final at Wimbledon in 1935 to the potent combination of Fred Perry and Dorothy Round. Hopman himself lost on a couple of occasions in the final of the Australian championship, as did his wife in 1939.

It was in 1950 that Harry became captain of the Australian Davis Cup team and the brilliant run of success began. He was a tactician, a disciplinarian and a practical psychologist, whose methods made enemies. In the Australian press his team was known as Hopman's Chain Gang. His wife was just as able an administrator. I first met her when she was chaperoning the formidable Little Mo Connolly around Europe in 1953. When she had to play Little Mo that year in an Australian tournament and wanted some practice with her husband, she found that he was coaching Little Mo!

Twelve years later she persuaded teams from ten countries to contest the women's Federation Cup in Melbourne. It was a great success, even at the financial level, and when the players stayed on for the Australian championships, these too made a profit for the first time for many years.

Frank Sedgman and Ken McGregor were the spearhead of Hopman's first team, with the precocious Hoad and Rosewall coming up fast on the rails. In the 1949 challenge round at Forest Hills, Ted

Schroeder and Pancho Gonzales were both too strong
for Sedgman, but the next year 23-year-old Sedgman
turned the tables, beating Schroeder and Brown, and
winning the doubles with John Bromwich.

It was only when Sedgman turned professional in
1953 that the Americans were briefly given a chance.
With Ken McGregor he formed a magnificent doubles
team, which achieved the Grand Slam of the four
chief men's tournaments in 1951.

McGregor's first selection for the challenge round
in 1950, at the relatively late age of twenty-six, flut-
tered the dovecots in Australia, since he was preferred
to such as John Bromwich. Harry Hopman, however,
knew what he was about. He knew that McGregor
was a man to rise to the occasion, a quality he had
shown when playing Australian Rules football before
he displayed it on the tennis court. This he duly did
again, beating Ted Schroeder in the opening singles,
and giving Australia a flying start. Six feet three inches
tall, McGregor, a splendidly fluent mover, had a service to match his deadly volleying, with ground
strokes to match the two. He was an admirable singles
player and perhaps better still in doubles. He won the
Australian singles title in 1952, having been runner-
up to Dick Savitt at Wimbledon the previous year.

It was in 1952 that two players even better than
these emerged at Wimbledon. Lew Hoad and Ken
Rosewall were only seventeen years old when
they gave a dazzling exhibition in the doubles, eli-
minating the favoured Americans, Dick Savitt and
Gardnar Mulloy. The same year, Hopman had them
both in the Davis Cup team, where they shone until
they turned professional in 1956 and 1957. Thus, they
were only in the 'real', supposedly amateur, game for

a few brief years, but in that time the impact they made was tremendous.

There could scarcely have been a greater physical contrast. Hoad was blond and enormously strong, Rosewall dark and slight. Hoad lived on his stupendous service and fearsome volleying, Rosewall on his perfect ground strokes, his nimbleness of foot, his expert strategy. When they played each other, it was an exquisite contrast of styles. They first met when they were only twelve years old, Rosewall wiping the floor with Hoad 6–0, 6–0 in the New South Wales schoolboy championships. Thereafter, apart from a short spell in the 1950s, he surprisingly maintained his advantage. In 1956 Hoad won the French, Australian and Wimbledon titles, beating Rosewall in Australia and England, but failing to beat him in the American final at Forest Hills.

Rosewall, 5 feet 6½ inches tall, was no mean volleyer and his service has perhaps been made out to be weaker than it was. There seems to have been little significant difference in pace from that of another distinguished little Australian, his successor, Rod Laver, who was certainly never accused of serving feebly. Though Rosewall played so many fine, exciting games and shots at Wimbledon, where he would reach a final as late as 1970, none was more dramatic than that with which he saved match point against Savitt and Mulloy in 1952. He and Hoad had been lobbed from the net, but Rosewall, dashing back full pelt, reached the ball, scorned the possibility of a lob of his own, and belted it on the backhand, straight between the astonished Americans.

Rosewall's father actually owned tennis courts in the Sydney suburb of Rockdale, where he taught his

son to play from the age of five. When he realized that
Ken was unlikely ever to be large, he cleverly
modelled his game accordingly, encouraging him to
rely on craft, control and precision. Devoted practice,
which began almost in infancy with hitting a ball
against a wall, and an admirable temperament did the
rest. With Rosewall, an engagingly boyish figure, there
were no excesses on court, just an amiable grin and a
desire to get on with the game.

1953 was a splendid year for Rosewall. He and Lew
Hoad won the Australian doubles championship, then
descended on Europe. In Paris, Rosewall achieved his
first major triumph, reaching the final to defeat Vic
Seixas, then ranked number four in the world. The
doubles championship with Hoad rounded off an
immensely profitable visit. Next came the Wimbledon
doubles, again in partnership with Hoad, the other
Australian pair of Rex Hartwig and Mervyn Rose
being their victims. Finally, they represented Australia
against America in the Davis Cup challenge round
and prevailed, after an uneasy start.

After being two to one sets down, Hoad splendidly
defeated Tony Trabert in five sets, which meant that
Ken Rosewall had to repeat his Parisian success over
Seixas to keep the cup. This he duly did, winning
6–2, 2–6, 6–3, 6–4. At the end of the year he was number two in the world, with Hoad at number five.

The following year he reached the first of his Wimbledon finals, only to be beaten by the crowd's beloved
Drobny.

Drobny could scarcely be begrudged his victory.
He had been competing at Wimbledon since 1938
when he was seventeen years old and he had found
time in the interim to win a silver medal for ice

hockey with the Czech Olympic team at St Moritz ten years later. Runner-up at Wimbledon in 1949 and 1952, in 1953 he and Budge Patty were locked in combat for four hours and twenty minutes, playing ninety-three games, in the course of which Drob saved no fewer than six match points. The penalty was a ruptured blood vessel in his leg.

The following year, much to his displeasure, Drob was seeded number eleven. Perhaps that gave him the fire and the incentive at last to take the title. Certainly it allowed him to make steady progress in decent obscurity. Budge Patty fell to him in the semi-final, and in the two days before the final he did everything he could to relax, down to fishing in his father-in-law's lake. He and Rosewall played a memorable match; two fine players who were outstanding sportsmen. Drob took the first set 13–11, Rosewall fought back to win the second 6–4, but Drobny, to the joy of the Centre Court spectators, won the next two and that elusive title. It is strange to think that, in future years, that same crowd would be willing Rosewall to the success he never had; not least in 1970 when, as a 35-year-old, he went down in the final to his compatriot John Newcombe.

Snubbed by the British Lawn Tennis Association when he volunteered to coach the Davis Cup team gratis, Drob took his huge experience and his flair for teaching to Italy, Sweden and South Africa, to impressive effect. In 1959 he ceased to be an honorary Englishman and became one officially, by naturalization.

As for Rosewall, there was a further disappointment to come when he and Lew Hoad surprisingly lost the Davis Cup to the Americans in Sydney; though they would regain it with a shattering 5–0 win at

Forest Hills the following year. 1956 saw Rosewall lose
his second Wimbledon final to Hoad; then came the
professional years.

The advent of open tennis, of which Australia, with
the Iron Curtain countries, had long been an opponent, enabled Rosewall to delight Wimbledon again.
As a professional he had much more success than
Hoad, who suffered many ailments and eventually
opened a tennis 'ranch' in Spain. Till Rod Laver
turned pro in 1963, Rosewall ruled the roost. 1968 saw
him back, after so many years, to win the British Hard
Courts title at Bournemouth, which was the first of
all open tournaments. Shamateurism was dead at last;
the true professional could compete with those who
had lived in a grey world of paid 'amateurism', and
who was a more fitting player than Ken Rosewall to
win the first trophy of the new era?

In 1970 he was good enough to win the American
singles again after a gap of fourteen years, but Wimbledon again slipped from his grasp. He took John
Newcombe, so much taller, heftier and younger,
to five tense sets, winning the first and fourth, but
tiring to lose 1–6 in the decider. At Forest Hills he
beat still another Australian star in the sturdy, left-
handed Tony Roche.

Lew Hoad's five-set victory over Tony Trabert
turned the 1953 Davis Cup in Australia's favour and
established him as a player of the highest potential.
His luck, however, never matched his talent. The next
two years saw him suffer from food poisoning, an eye
injury and trouble with his back. Gradually he fought
his way through, tightened up his already powerful
game, and was rewarded in 1956. As we have seen, only
Ken Rosewall at Forest Hills robbed him of the Grand

Slam. In 1957 he took Wimbledon again, this time
with an easy victory in the final against his fellow
Australian Ashley Cooper. It took him less than an
hour. A couple of days later he, too, turned professional under the aegis of Jack Kramer. It took him but
a year and a half to earn the £48,000 Jack Kramer had
guaranteed him in two years, but continuing back
trouble marred his years as a professional.

By now, as you will have noted, there was a serious
distortion in the international tennis game. The best
players, like Gonzales in his time, were turning overtly
professional very young. Increasingly, the 'amateur'
game was being left with only its hypocrisy and its
lesser lights. It was this, more than anything else,
which whittled away the prestige and validity of the
Davis Cup. Open tennis restored the possibility of the
best players competing; but now there was so much
money to be won, so many calls on time and travel,
that the stars were not always interested. Patriotism
often came second to the demands of the Grand Tour
and the process was self-perpetuating.

Little Mo and Others

Before Tracy Austin there was Maureen Connolly –
not quite as young when she achieved her stunning
successes, but very young indeed, for all that. Ebullient, engaging, enormously determined, 'Little Mo'
conquered and captivated Wimbledon as a teenager,
but was to die pitifully young.

She was ten years old when she began to play on the
public playground just down the road in San Diego.
Curiously, she was a natural left-hander, but was persuaded to change to a right-handed grip because there
had never been a major woman left-hander. Certainly
it did her no harm. By the time she was twelve, she
came under the aegis of the phenomenally successful
Californian coach, Eleanor 'Teach' Tennant, who had
previously coached Bobby Riggs and Alice Marble,
thus bringing up a distinguished double at Wimbledon in 1939.

Eleanor Tennant not only attended to the funda-
mentals of Maureen Connolly's game, but also had her
dancing and skipping to increase her agility. She was
only fourteen when she won the American junior title,
sixteen when she won the senior title, seventeen when
she won Wimbledon. She won the Grand Slam in
1953 and took two more Wimbledon titles in a row,
losing less then twenty games in the second and third
years of her triumphs there. Her four-year Wightman

Cup record was a hundred per cent, while between 1952 and 1954 she was beaten only four times.

'My aim,' she said once, 'is to perfect my tennis; then, if I perfect my tennis, I will beat everyone.' Her powers of concentration were quite extraordinary; before her matches she would almost go into a trance, and after one of her Wimbledon triumphs she went off to knock-up on an outer court. Though she was a tiny girl, her ground strokes were extremely strong and she welded on to them a net game which, if it did not come naturally to her, was still highly effective and made her still less beatable. Perhaps, given the depth of her determination, it was inevitable that she would fall out with the demanding 'Teach' Tennant, and this she did at the delicate moment of her first tournament at Wimbledon.

Her nickname was given her by an American journalist friend who compared her with the battleship *Missouri*. It seemed she must dominate women's tennis for years to come, but tragic times lay ahead. In 1954 when out riding – her other great passion – in San Diego, a cement lorry banged into her, horribly injuring her right leg. The appalling damage to the main artery and to the muscles were such that her tennis career was over. Bravely she made the best of it, marrying that year the Olympic athlete Norman Brinker, later bringing up two children and becoming a successful writer and commentator on the game. Alas, she would live only another fifteen years after her accident; cancer killed her in 1969, still only in her middle thirties. One remembers her fresh, bright, endearing youthfulness on that European tour of 1953, with Nell Hopman and the Californian player Julie Sansom. It is still hard to reconcile all that exuberant precocity, that early achievement, with the sombre things that lay ahead.

In her three Wimbledon finals, Little Mo twice beat Louise Brough, once Doris Hart. In 1957 and 1958 the title went to Althea Gibson, a strong, lanky Negress whose father had once contemplated making her a professional boxer, but whose athletic aggression found its outlet on the tennis court. She was the first black player to win a major tennis title and was helped to overcome her own poverty and the prejudices of the time by a series of generous benefactors. Born in South Carolina, brought up in New York, cutting her teeth on paddle tennis, she affirmed her quality at Forest Hills in 1950, when she gave Louise Brough a terrible fright. In 1957 and 1958 she won that title too.

She had an excellent service, a strong volley, and an eye for a ball which allowed her – like so many other tennis stars – to become a very good golfer. She was not graceful to watch, but there is no doubt she was exceedingly effective. As Wimbledon champion she succeeded the resourceful Shirley Fry, one of the best doubles players as well as one of the leading singles players of her American generation.

There could scarcely have been a more contrasting figure with Miss Gibson than Angela Mortimer, the English girl whom she beat in the Paris final of 1956, and again in the Wimbledon final of 1958. Miss Mortimer would have abundant consolation when she won the title herself three years later, the first English girl to do so since Dorothy Round twenty-one years before.

Where Miss Gibson was tough, Miss Mortimer was genteel. Where Miss Gibson had grown up largely

in the slums of Manhattan, Miss Mortimer came
from the tranquil county of Devon. She was one of
the several successful pupils of a distinguished
original coach, Arthur Roberts, who used the courts
of the Palace Hotel, Torquay, to instruct his pro-
tégés. They included his own son, Paddy, an able
player; Mike Sangster, one of the best English singles
players since the war, and Sue Barker, who was lucky
enough to be at her peak when huge sums were
there to be won.

Angela Mortimer was never, perhaps, an exciting
player to watch, but she was a very good one, with
an imposing record. Her service was her weakest
point. She was never very strong, but her ground
strokes were excellent, and she was an outstanding
strategist. The brashness and histrionics of so many
later stars were not for her; one remembers her,
when not on court, sitting quietly in some corner
reading a novel. In 1955, at twenty-three, she won
the Paris singles final against America's Dorothy
Knode; in 1958 the Australian championship with
a straight-sets win against Lorraine Coghlan; and, of
course, in 1961, Wimbledon.

If one's sympathies went out that rainy afternoon,
to Christine Truman, who slipped on the wet turf,
crashed to the ground, and limped through a match
she had seemed so sure to win, Miss Mortimer, too,
had her difficulties. Much pain from a tennis elbow
had led her to enter Wimbledon only, so she thought,
to make sure she could watch it from the competitors' seats. This may, ironically, have taken off the
pressure and helped her to her notable success.

Christine Truman took the first set of that final
6–4, and looked on the way to a comfortable victory,

deploying her far superior strength and exploiting her youth. It was a net cord that undid her and indirectly decided the game. She turned sharply, fell heavily, badly hurt her leg, and limped through the rest of the match. A heavy girl 6 feet tall, and never especially mobile at the best of times, it was cruel now to see her struggling to reach the ball. Still, she made a game of it, losing the second set by 6–4, the third set 7–5.

There can be little doubt that in normal circumstances it would have been her Wimbledon. Still, she was only twenty, experience seemed likely to mitigate her faults, give her the consistency she missed, and make her, eventually, a champion. Alas, no. Never again did she get to a Wimbledon final. Nor would she ever again reach the final at Forest Hills, where she had been runner-up two years before, the year she won her solitary major title in Paris.

Christine Truman – Janes when she married – was at once a maddening and a thoroughly endearing figure. An Essex girl from Woodford, she was almost the archetype of a John Betjeman heroine – muscular, athletic, yet unspoiled and charming. In an age when the talk was increasingly of 'aggression' and 'killer instinct' as laudable qualities, she – and Angela Mortimer – proved that success did not always go to the ruthless.

Yet her success, as I have said, should have been so much greater. Her suburban upbringing, her endlessly present, watchful mother who could be seen at her tournaments, and her sense of proportion may to some degree have been her undoing. Success in international tennis, as her successor, Virginia

Wade, would find, seems to be possible only at the expense of absolute commitment. After the 1961 Wimbledon, she surprisingly lost a vital singles in the Wightman Cup to Karen Hantze and announced that she was going to retire: at twenty. There was gloom all around, and not only in Britain. Miss Truman thought again and changed her mind. She said she would not do it again. 'I felt I was wasting time to go on,' she explained to me at that juncture, 'and I don't like to waste time. I'd rather get on and do something else. I hate having anything on my mind like that. I never thought that so many people would be so interested. I was flattered. I like to have things sorted out in my mind, not muddled. I couldn't say: one, two, three, these are the reasons. It was a number of things that seemed to come up at the time. I thought, after the American trip, I can't finish on a bad note like that.' Nor did she, even if her promise never came fully to fruition.

There were times, watching her strike her service, with its tremendous power, watching her thump her devastating smashes, an irresistible giantess, that you would wonder how any girl could beat her. There were other times, as double fault succeeded double fault, when you wondered if she would ever cease to be erratic. 'I think it's sometimes when I'm winning and I've got a lead,' she said. 'I seem to be doing all right, and unconsciously I relax. Before I know where I am, I've made a few silly mistakes, and I've lost the game. Sometimes I'm better when I'm down. I realize I've got to do something, and I pull myself round.'

She went on playing for another eight years, always the darling of the courts, but with never quite the

same power. Her highest ranking was second in the
world in 1959; she made no fewer than ten appearances in the Wightman Cup, the first as a seventeen-
year-old in 1958. That was the year when she helped
Britain to a famous 4–3 victory, defeating both Althea
Gibson and Dorothy Knode in the singles. It was
Britain's first success since 1930.

1961 was the year that Billie Jean Moffitt, later
King, made her début at Wimbledon, and in which
Bobby Wilson, as tantalizing and suburban as Chris-
tine Truman in his way, played perhaps the best
tennis of his career when he knocked the holder,
Australia's Neal Fraser, out of the tournament on the
Centre Court.

Billie Jean arrived in England as an ebullient and
refreshing seventeen-year-old, with a beguiling, ir-
reverent approach to the game. 'Don't applaud: just
throw dollars and cents!' she would cry on the court
at some staid tournament. Yet when she got to Wimbledon and the Centre Court, it was too much for her.
Nervousness reduced her to a jelly, and she made
feeble resistance to the sturdy, attractive little Mexi-
can, Yola Ramirez, who beat her with ease. Did it,
as the saying goes, kill something fine in her? True,
she had abundant consolation when she and Karen
Hantze, unseeded teenagers, took the doubles title,
but the memory of that humiliating afternoon on the
Centre Court must have lingered. The fearsomely
competitive, muttering, sometimes snarling Billie Jean
King of the seventies was hardly to be seen or predicted in the cheerful, thick-legged, bespectacled girl
of 1961.

Another Californian, whose brother was a base-
ball star, Billie Jean – another irony – took to tennis

at the age of eleven because she thought it was a lady-like game. A natural serve and volley player, she complemented this with a precocious strategic flair, and in 1960 she already ranked fourth in the States. More of her later.

Bobby Wilson came from Finchley in North London, worked in the tyre business, and appalled the committed and the competitive by continuing, even as a star, to practise with his mother on the local tennis club courts. Had Wilson been a Californian ... But why speculate? He was not, any more than he had the ruthless drive of a Perry. Wilson was slender, an Austin rather than a Perry, prevailing through technique, not power. Unlike Austin, however, he was often in hot water, locking horns with the tennis authorities even in the year he beat Fraser. His nonchalant attitude after he had lost an indoor match against France led, for a time, to his being cast out into the cold, which was as great a punishment for British tennis as it was for Wilson.

I was lucky enough to see him beat Fraser in an early round at Wimbledon in 1961. His recovery was quite extraordinary, seeming to give the lie to those who had always impugned his tenacity, rather than his unquestioned skill. Fraser annihilated him in the opening set 6–1, when we suffered with him, stroke by inadequate stroke. Then something happened. What odds would even the most cautious of bookmakers have given against the next set going, as it did, 6–0 to Wilson? His slight figure, thin white scarf knotted at the neck – more Petticoat Lane than Wimbledon – resisted, persisted and prevailed. Fraser, in the white floppy hat Australian cricketers and tennis players like, lolloped doggedly about the court, but could not resist him. It was, with all deference to Wilson, a reminder that Kramer – who had unsuccessfully tried to make him turn professional the year before – had creamed off most of the players who truly mattered.

Wilson did not win Wimbledon that year or any other. The closest he came to a title was in 1960 when, with Mike Davies, a useful British player who turned pro and ultimately became an administrator, he reached the final of the Wimbledon doubles, losing to Ralston and Osuna. On wood, he was excellent, winning the King's Cup, a respectable European international tournament, three times in a row with the British team between 1967 and 1970, while he won the British Covered Courts title three times.

It was a solid record, but probably did not express his full potential. He turned down professionalism, he once told me, 'Because I rather like to play my tennis when and where I wish. In the light of how things have turned out since,' – he was referring to the contretemps after the match against France – 'it seems that you can't play when and where you wish, even as an amateur.'

Twenty-seven at the time, he was still talking about improving his game. 'I'm sure I can improve,' he said. 'I think I've got a lot to learn. I feel that each season I'm playing a little better; I don't know whether it's the fact that other people are playing a little bit worse. I've got more idea of the game, more shots, and there are a lot of shots I don't play enough of. For instance, my lobbing is very poor. Often when I try for a passing shot, when he's sitting on the net, I know full well if only I'd lobbed him, I'd have won the point. And passing shots: often I'd take a swipe at the ball when I didn't have to.'

Mike Sangster and Yorkshire's Roger Taylor, a stalwart left-hander, were other English players of the period who had their crowded hours of glorious life, electrified Wimbledon for a match or two, but somehow couldn't sustain their best form.

Taylor could scarcely have been a greater contrast to Wilson. Where Wilson came from docile suburbia, Taylor was from the industrial north, the son of a steelworker, who was initially coached by his mother. Those Americans who are always telling the English that their players have had things too easy have not been obliged to struggle for time and space on public courts thronged with would-be Kramers and Connollys. They would doubtless have made an exception for Taylor, who came to London at sixteen, worked in a warehouse, played tennis how and where he could, 'bumming' his way around Britain to do so. On the Continent he travelled with a tent and a primus stove. He called, in those days, a spade a spade, and once had the better of a bout of dressing-room fisticuffs with the controversial Australian turned South African, Bob Hewitt.

A muscular left-hander with an excellent service, a fine forehand and a backhand which improved in time, Taylor excelled himself in the last all-amateur, or shamateur, Wimbledon of 1967, managing to reach the semi-finals; a feat he repeated in 1970, when he beat Rod Laver. In 1968 he joined the World Championship tennis group formed by the shy Texan millionaire, Lamar Hunt, who also owned American football and soccer franchises, and whose patronage, more even than the work of Kramer, would transform the position of the professional tennis player. In 1970 Taylor was ranked number eight in the world, though the only major final in which he ever figured was the mixed doubles championship of Australia in 1962, when he was runner-up with the blonde American Amazon, Darlene Hard, herself a singles finalist at Wimbledon.

Mike Sangster, the right-handed Devonian, another vigorous, well-built player, also had his jewelled moments at Wimbledon, though his most consistent success was attained in the King's Cup, a competition initiated by King Gustav V of Sweden which Great Britain won four times in the years from 1964 to 1967.

Meanwhile, there was Ann Haydon Jones, the Birmingham table tennis star turned tennis champion, a left-hander, strongly built and strongly determined, with a nice dry humour, great self-possession, and enough sheer talent and drive to win Wimbledon in 1969 with a magnificent three-set victory over Billie Jean King.

She reached the semi-final as early as 1962, when it seemed she would be the third English girl in the final in two years, but she lost to Karen Susman – née Hantze. With plans to marry Pip Jones, a man considerably older than herself, later in the year, she seemed weary of travel, and unlikely to go on playing with the same dedication and ambition. 'The travelling gets a bit wearying,' she admitted to me then. 'It's really these jets, because everything's speeding you up so. One day you're in the Caribbean, and the next you're in Monte Carlo, in the freezing cold, and they wonder why you get beaten. Living out of a suitcase all the time: you're staying in people's homes, say hello on the Monday morning when you unpack the suitcase, you're beginning to become a part of their life, and then on Sunday you pack your case and leave. Well, you have no roots, have you? That's the trouble.

Suzanne Lenglen won
Wimbledon six times between
1919 and 1925, thrilling the
crowds with her fluid
movements and fiery
temperament. *B.B.C. Hulton
Picture Library*

Helen Wills Moody (Little
Miss Poker Face) dominated
the women's game for
thirteen years. She won seven
American titles and was ladies
singles champion at
Wimbledon a record eight
times. *B.B.C. Hulton Picture
Library*

Maureen Connolly (*above*), receiving the ladies singles trophy at Wimbledon in 1954 from the Duchess of Kent. 'Little Mo' was a teenage phenomenon, winning her first major title at the age of sixteen. *Keystone*

Chris Lloyd, nicknamed the 'Ice Maiden' because of her composure on court, uses her double-fisted backhand to great effect. *Keystone*

Ann Haydon Jones (*opposite left*), one of the finest post-war players to emerge in England, climaxed her career by winning the ladies singles title at Wimbledon in 1969. *Keystone*

Billie Jean King (*opposite right*), a remarkable player with an impressive list of championships to her credit, has won a record twenty Wimbledon titles during her twenty-year career. *Keystone*

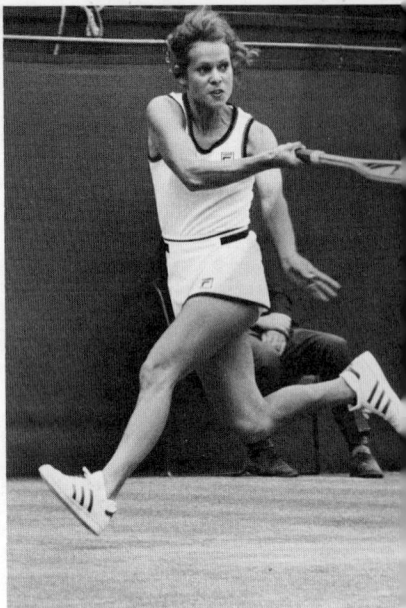

Evonne Cawley got off to a flying start in the 1979 Wimbledon championship but she did not regain the singles title she had first won nine years earlier till 1980. *Keystone*

Martina Navratilova playing in her opening match during the 1980 Wimbledon championship. She was unsuccessful in her attempt to win the singles title for the third year in a row. *Keystone*

R. F. and H. L. Doherty (Big Do and Little Do) were the Prince Charmings of tennis and dominated the game between 1897 and 1906. *B.B.C. Hulton Picture Library*

Bill Tilden, still regarded by many experts as the greatest player of all time, was invincible during the 1920s. His career spanned twenty-five years. *B.B.C. Hulton Picture Library*

Jean Borotra (*left*), the 'Bounding Basque', playing at Wimbledon in 1926. He learnt to play as a schoolboy in England and went on to win an impressive number of championships. *B.B.C. Hulton Picture Library*

Fred Perry (*below*), jumping the net after beating J. H. Crawford of Australia to win Wimbledon in 1936. A fast and elegant player, Perry was acknowledged by many as the best English player ever. *B.B.C. Hulton Picture Library*

H. W. 'Bunny' Austin (*left*) – a British player of great skill and technique – fighting it out against Don Budge (U.S.A.) in the 1938 singles final at Wimbledon. *B.B.C. Hulton Picture Library*

Rod Laver, four times singles champion at Wimbledon, seen in action on the Centre Court in 1977. He was the only man to bring off the Grand Slam twice. *Keystone*

Arthur Ashe (*below*), in action in the 1975 Wimbledon championship. He went on to play in a memorable final against Jimmy Connors and became the first black man to win Wimbledon. *Keystone*

John McEnroe, a temperamental player whose game is a mixture of delicacy and power, is seen here in a match leading to the riveting 1980 Wimbledon final against Borg. *Keystone*

Jimmy Connors (*below*), a gifted player who has won most of the major championships, was devotedly coached by his mother and grandmother. *Toby Glanville*

I'll go on playing until it loses its appeal for me. I suppose I haven't really thought about it. It doesn't do to think too much about the future; you make too many set plans, and then you've disappointed yourself.'

Of much the same persuasion was the towering Italian star, Orlando Sirola, who, with the chunkily-built, good-looking Roman, Nicola Pietrangeli, brought so much joy to the doubles courts of the world. At a time when tennis was becoming an increasingly grim affair – though nothing like as grim and frenetic as it is today – these two contributed to the gaiety of nations. They would fool about, kick tennis balls as though they were footballs, generally enjoy themselves, yet they achieved a remarkable amount of success, both in international tournaments and in the Davis Cup.

One wet afternoon at Queen's Club, in the midst of the pre-Wimbledon tournament, Sirola poured out his thoughts and his despair to me. Shamateurism displeased him, but it was inevitable, he thought, 'The day that man was made; it was decided when someone said, "I'm sure the caretaker could beat that man in flannels with a pipe," and the caretaker said afterwards, "Yes, but I've lost a day's work. Give me a pound!"'

Sirola was thirty-five by then, and he had had enough. Pietrangeli would go on to manage the Italian Davis Cup team through some controversial periods; but what Italian manager, in any sport, does not have them? Half cowboy hero, half clown, Sirola, who knocked out Mike Sangster in 1963, admitted, with a smile that charmed and belied what he said, that tennis had become a trial. 'I'm only happy at home. I work, go home, take off my shoes, have the television on, and the children. Here, you're in the middle of people with whom you've nothing in common. "Good morning, how are you, pity you didn't win yesterday." What can I talk to them about? I also believe that this game, with its terrific tensions, somehow crushes the personality of the players, it tends to bring everybody down to the same level.

'At bottom, this is a game. One must always put it in its proper, photographic perspective. It's not life; it's a part of life. But there isn't even an intellectual level among them; not from a cultural point of view, but from the aspect of pure intelligence. If there were, they would get some benefit from what happens to them, but it just isn't there.' He complained, too, of what he called 'the drama of tennis; you can't see what you want to see. We see nothing of the world, nothing. A journalist who goes to report the Davis Cup and stays three days will see much more; more than us who stay there a month.'

Great stars with overwhelming personalities were, he felt, a thing of the past. 'When you played against von Cramm, it was like playing against a mountain. Flam, Larsen, Patty – all of them were extremely powerful and imposing personalities who made a player feel inferior. So was Hoad – a most impressive personality. I'm sure that half Patty's opponents were physically superior to him, but he managed to put them into such a state of subjection that he beat them. Now, I couldn't even tell you one player with an outstanding personality.'

Sirola and Pietrangeli twice took Italy to the challenge round of the Davis Cup. Pietrangeli, much the better singles player, was in fact born in Tunis, his father French, his mother Russian, and not till 1960 – having been brought up in Rome – did he finally acquire Italian nationality. His ground strokes were exemplary, and had he possessed a decent service, he might have been among the most successful players of his time. He did win the French championship in 1959 and in 1960, the year in which he accepted a three-year $50,000 contract from Jack Kramer – what small beer it seems now – only to give the money back the very next day. There was, he said, no atmosphere in pro tennis; he wanted to tell his children and grandchildren about the Davis Cup and Wimbledon. It would be another eight years before the international tennis authorities made such quixotic considerations irrelevant.

Though Hoad and Rosewall were among the pros, it was the Australians who now dominated tennis even if, until the emergence of Rod Laver, they were not quite of the first flight. Ashley Cooper beat Neale Fraser for the Wimbledon title in 1958. Fraser took it two years later, beating Laver in the final. Laver came into his own in the next two years. Roy Emerson was successful in 1964 and 1965, John Newcombe in 1967. Two more titles for Laver and another for John Newcombe followed that.

The retirement from amateur tennis of Lew Hoad left the way clear for the handsome Ashley Cooper to thrive and prosper before following Hoad, a year later, into professionalism. Brought up in Melbourne, taught by his father to play tennis at the age of ten, soon taken up by Harry Hopman, Cooper was a very strong player with an outstanding backhand and a fine reputation for sportsmanship. Hoad made a meal of him in the 1957 Wimbledon final, and even though

Hoad had now turned pro he failed in the final at Forest Hills as well, going down to another compatriot in Mal Anderson.

1958, however, saw everything come together. Only the French title eluded him as he beat Fraser in the final at Wimbledon, had his revenge on Anderson in the final at Forest Hills, and won the Australian title into the bargain. His years of professionalism were, alas, cut short by an unusual injury to his arm.

Neale Fraser, too, had physical difficulties; in his case, varicose veins, which were finally cured by an operation. He seemed perpetually in the wars. In 1960, the year of his success at Wimbledon, he had to be carried off the Stade Roland Garros in the French championship with cramp; the year before he had made light of a grumbling appendix when winning all his Davis Cup matches for Australia against America, and had brought off a treble in the American championships.

A left-hander, his strength lay in his perfectly calibrated service and his effective volleying. On the ground his forehand was a strong one, but his backhand, much exploited by Ashley Cooper in the Wimbledon final in 1958, was far less robust.

Fraser started to play tennis at the age of eleven, at the same time as his brother John, who was another talented performer, but they were *not* taught by their father, a High Court judge. Ranked the best in the world in 1959 and 1960, rewarded for his persistence in trying to improve that vulnerable backhand, Fraser refused the blandishments of professionalism, but he too saw his later career undermined by physical ailments. Two more operations took the edge off his game, but after his retirement he remained in tennis, succeeding Harry Hopman as manager of the Australian Davis Cup team.

His partner in doubles, where he had so much success, was often his fellow Australian, Roy Emerson, for whom the way to success was opened when Rod Laver turned pro in 1963. Emerson himself stayed an amateur for another five years, and played in nine consecutive Davis Cup challenge rounds. His record was the extraordinary one of a single defeat in a dozen singles rubbers, two defeats in half a dozen doubles.

Born in 1936 on a dairy farm in Queensland, Emerson used to say that it was a long time before he had hit more tennis balls than he had milked cows. He was a humorous fellow. Once, looking out from the competitors' lounge at a women's tennis match, he mused sardonically on the proliferation of lobs; there, he said, was a lobbed forehand, there a lobbed backhand, there a lobbed service, culminating in the final ignominy – a lobbed smash!

An excellent athlete as a schoolboy and always outstandingly fit. Emerson did come from a tennis-playing family, one with its own court, and he won his first tournament at eleven. So keen was his father on Roy becoming a crack player that he moved the whole family to Brisbane, then allowed his son to leave school at seventeen. The gamble paid. Emerson won every single major title: Wimbledon in 1964 and 1965, Forest Hills in 1961 and 1964, the French championship in 1963 and 1967, the Australian no fewer than half a dozen times – the last five in a row.

There was no special weakness in Emerson's game, but he was particularly strong on the backhand and his service, after a somewhat bizarre wind-up, was

forceful and accurate. In two of his Wimbledon finals
he beat the 'eternal second', the tall, blond, agreeable
Fred Stolle, a fellow Australian who had been runner-
up to America's stalwart, high-pitched Chuck
McKinley in 1963.

Time and time again, the left-handed Stolle found
himself the runner-up, but he did win the American
championship in 1966 and the French in 1965. He
was an excellent doubles player too, winning the
mixed title at Wimbledon in 1961 and 1964 with
Lesley Turner, the men's with Bob Hewitt in 1962
and 1964, and many other titles besides. On the subject of his amateur status, he tended to be wry and
ironic. He turned full professional in 1966, and eventually came to rest in the United States as a tennis
club pro in Miami.

Looking back on that epoch, one recalls a sense of
great frustration. The ostrich posture of the I.L.T.F.,
the continuing dichotomy between shamateurism –
you could scarcely pretend to call it amateurism – and
Kramer's professional 'circus' robbed the major tournaments of their reality, though 'expenses' paid to
players at them zoomed up year by year. Wimbledon
itself – the All England Club – came out of the sorry
affair with great credit. It wanted to go 'open', although with spectators clamouring every year for
tickets, and with huge sums returned annually to the
unsuccessful, it could easily have stayed as it was. One
had the impression at the time that the crowds would
keep thronging to the tournament for its gilded fort-
night even if two public park players were to be seen
on the Centre Court. Of one of those Emerson–Stolle
finals I remarked at the time that it reminded me of
André Gide's response to the question, who was the

best French poet? 'Victor Hugo, alas.' These were two admirable competitors, but the true talent was elsewhere.

This was not so – at least for the moment – in women's tennis, where matters were a good deal more satisfactory. For a little while the Australian–American dominance was broken by, of all people, a Brazilian – Maria Bueno. A handful of players, such as the Kochs, had come out of Brazil, but Bueno was the first major figure to emerge from that huge country. Moreover, in an epoch when the serve-and-volley Californian girls and the Australians were bestriding women's tennis, it was splendid to watch so slender and graceful a player prevail.

A native of São Paolo, daughter of a veterinary dietician who insisted she qualify as a schoolteacher and not merely play tennis, she was good enough at fourteen to take a set from the formidable Shirley Fry. The double strain of study and tennis caused her to lose more than a stone in one month, but in 1958, still aged only nineteen, she was able to set out on her first European tour, winning the Italian title in Rome at the Foro Italico, and the Wimbledon doubles. Her measured ground strokes, her crisp volleying, her boundless determination, and her flowing movement made her a joy to watch and a terror to play. In 1959 she won the Wimbledon final in straight sets against the American, Darlene Hard.

In the 1960 Wimbledon singles final she was far too good in the end for the pretty South African girl, Sandra Reynolds, who could produce a mighty forehand out of all proportion to her shape and size. Miss Bueno had trouble with that forehand in the first set, which she won only by 8–6, but the steam had gone out of Miss Reynolds and she lost the second set to love.

After four and a half months in bed with hepatitis in 1964, Miss Bueno steadily returned to her commanding heights. She did still better at Forest Hills than at Wimbledon, winning the singles no fewer than four times: in 1959, 1963, 1964 and 1966. Wimbledon she took again in 1964, beating hefty Margaret Smith (later Court) of Australia in three sets. The following year Margaret Smith had her revenge in straight sets, and in 1966, reaching the final for the third year in a row, Miss Bueno went down in three sets to Billie Jean King.

São Paolo was ecstatic about her success. In 1959 they flew her home from England in a private aeroplane, drove her through Rio in triumph, celebrated mass for her in São Paolo cathedral, and put up a sixty-foot statue to commemorate her success. Trouble with her knee and the familiar tennis elbow sabotaged her in 1968 and 1969; she was never again to be the same captivating player.

The first of Maria Bueno's Wimbledon finals against Margaret Smith was an extraordinary one, full of bizarre changes of fortune, sudden upheavals, unforced mistakes, brilliant recoveries and unexpected failings. Watching, one might have known it would be odd when, in the very first game, Margaret Smith, the champion, lost her powerful service, promptly taking Miss Bueno's to love. Miss Bueno went on to win that set 6–4, but in the second her whiplash elegance seemed no match for the strength and gymnastic resilience of Miss Smith, who went into a 4–0 lead.

The Latin temperament, however, is infinitely mercurial. If Miss Smith had conquered the ravages of temperament she showed in the first set, then Miss Bueno displayed a rubber-ball resilience. By returning from a double fault on game point in the fourth game, she promptly took Miss Smith's service when the Australian herself double-faulted twice, and eventually went down by only 9–7. She was in the groove again, broke Miss Smith's service at 4–3, re-established her early superiority, and ran out 6–3 in the final set.

Competitive tennis has always been a battle of wits, nerves and presence. Christine Truman, herself no lightweight, once admitted that when she faced Margaret Smith across the net at Wimbledon she thought forebodingly to herself, 'Gosh, she looks fit!' Indeed Miss Smith was fit. She trained with weights, once told an impressed British journalist, on the dance floor, that she could lift 160 lbs, and her grip was crushingly strong.

Her career was one of huge achievement and early precocity, strangely chequered by lapses. She was no large, inanimate lump but a sensitive young woman whose vulnerability was often her undoing. An early sign of this was given at the age of seventeen in 1960, when within a matter of days she lost the Australian junior singles final to little Lesley Turner, won the senior championship, then lost the local club championship to a woman twice her age in straight sets, going down to love in the second!

Born in Albery, New South Wales, her early passion for the game had her sneaking on to the local courts with young friends, hoping the keeper would not spot them; which he did only when the ball was allowed to pass Margaret at the net. So good a quarter- and half-miler was she that coaches wanted her to become an athlete, with an eye on the Olympics, but she preferred tennis, and at twelve years old was already winning tournaments, though she never did win the national junior title.

Various coaches played their part: Wal Rutter first, an Albery man who nobly passed her on to Frank Sedgman, Ken Rogers and the physical fitness expert, Stan Nicholls, in Melbourne. Though an amateur in name, she led the life of a full-time athlete – on the courts, in the gymnasium and out running twice a week with a women's athletics club.

Her first visit to Europe was in 1961 at eighteen. Ann Haydon beat her in the French championships, and Christine Truman, for all Margaret's imposing appearance of fitness, beat her at Wimbledon. In 1962, however, she came back to win in Paris, Lesley Turner being her victim, and to be top seed at Wimbledon where she crashed out to Billie Jean King, eternal rival, in her very first game. 1963 saw her win Wimbledon, still only twenty years old, with the satisfaction of beating Billie Jean King in the final in straight sets. She would beat her again to take the American title two years later. But in 1963 the tensions of tennis worked on her, and after several uneasy if intermittently successful years, she gave it up in 1966 at only twenty-four.

It could hardly last. Marriage to Barry Court, an international yachtsman, doubtless helped her; he encouraged her to come back to the game, and this she did after training in secret. In the meantime she had made herself into an excellent squash player. In 1969 she was back at her best, or – in the opinion of some experts – even better. She won three of the main championships, failing only at Wimbledon, where Ann Haydon Jones, at the top of her game, knocked her out in a thrilling semi-final. Again she said she would retire, but only partially. There was no better woman player of her era, and none better ever came out of Australia.

Confidence surely played a part and made some of the difference in the two Wimbledon finals between Billie Jean King and Ann Haydon Jones. Billie Jean won the first in straight sets in 1967, but two years later, when she seemed in clear sight of success, the tables were turned. Ann Haydon Jones, nervous and under pressure from the expectations of the Wimbledon crowd, lost the first set 6–3, was forty–love down in the fourth game of the second set, and serving. She saved those three points, won the game, the set and eventually the match, 3–6, 6–3, 6–2.

Though at the age of eleven Ann Haydon Jones was told she could never play any sport, being bedridden for months with a kidney complaint, her father, an international table tennis player, persuaded her to take up table tennis. This the left-handed Ann did with such splendid results that in 1957, the year she turned nineteen, she was runner-up in the singles, doubles and mixed doubles for the world titles. It was the beginning of her strange 'always a bridesmaid, never a bride' experience. She was half a dozen times a semi-finalist, and once a beaten finalist at Wimbledon, before she ultimately took the title – to which she added the 1961 and 1966 French championships. Even in these, she was three times runner-up.

The slower surface suited her patient play, though by the late sixties, when she was using a metal racket and had turned professional, she was a far more versatile player.

After her triumph at Wimbledon, the blonde Birmingham girl had trouble with her shoulder. By October she had given up her professional contract and in 1970, though she played for the Wightman Cup team, she did not defend her title. She had won it just in time.

Rod Laver and the Monstrous Regiment

Rod Laver, the only man to bring off the Grand Slam twice – in 1962 and 1969 – is regarded by some critics as the finest tennis player of all time. That must ultimately be a matter of opinion, but his claims are manifest. In all, he won Wimbledon four times, Forest Hills twice, the French championship twice, the Australian three times, while he figured in a string of successful Australian Davis Cup teams, the first in 1959, the last as late as 1973 when he was thirty-five. Not much larger than his compatriot Ken Rosewall, whom he would catch up with on the professional tour, he was a left-hander who conquered the left-hander's problem of a vulnerable backhand, hit a swift forehand and a notable service return, and compounded all this with intense perfectionism and immense mobility.

In his prime he was a quiet, compact, remote little man, yet on the court his personality was in essence an adventurous one: he went for winners. Jack Kramer's calculating stance was quite foreign to him; scorning safety first, he hit shots which were sometimes difficult, sometimes even risky, usually bringing them off. His eye was superb, his speed unusual. Five feet $8\frac{1}{2}$ inches tall, weighing about 10 st 7 lbs (68 kg), he could sweep much larger men off the court.

Laver, like Roy Emerson, with whom he won the

Australian doubles in his second Grand Slam year, was born on an Australian farm – in his case, one in Queensland. When the family moved ninety miles from Langdale to Rockworth, it perhaps became inevitable that he would in due course gain the nickname of Rod the Rocket.

It may be an apocryphal tale that he became so fast because, having battered the fence with tennis balls, he was obliged to build one of his own, which was so rickety that the ball came off at all sorts of strange angles. What is certain is that in Rockworth he came under a coach called Charlie Hollis, who played a major part in his career by teaching him a topspin backhand. Now dipping, now rising high on the bounce, it would be a notable weapon.

For once we have a great tennis player who was not a prodigy, though he did develop very quickly in his late teens. He was picked for his first tour abroad at eighteen, when there were still four junior players ranked ahead of him. Victory in the junior Forest Hills tournament and second place at junior Wimbledon showed what he might do. In 1959 he did it.

Wimbledon saw him reach all three finals. He lost to Alex Olmedo in the men's singles, winning only the mixed doubles with Darlene Hard, but his quality was established beyond doubt. Olmedo, a Peruvian who the previous year, at twenty-two, had been controversially picked for the American Davis Cup team, beating Cooper and Anderson in Brisbane to restore the trophy to the States, was an accomplished serve-and-volley man.

Olmedo had already won the Australian title at the expense of Neale Fraser when he met Laver at Wimbledon, beating him in straight sets. He would beat

Laver again in the 1959 Davis Cup challenge round, though Australia ran out winners as Fraser defeated him in his other singles. That December, Olmedo became a professional, and a substantial obstacle was out of Laver's way.

Not that he would not have negotiated it in his own good time. He was the beaten finalist again at Wimbledon in 1960, this time being beaten in four sets by Neale Fraser – he took the second set, 6–3 – but the next two years saw him champion.

He had learned to husband his resources. Meeting him that year at the pleasant Hurlingham Club tournament in south-west London, one heard that Laver would not be taking part in the Wimbledon mixed doubles, even though he enjoyed them.

'I like to play mixed; that's probably my downfall. We have lots of rallies; it's very interesting, I think. With a lady player, you have to work things out.' In that Hurlingham tournament, a solid English player called Alan Mills knocked the coming Wimbledon champion out of the singles in the semi-final. 'Well, it doesn't mean anything, you see,' Laver explained, after an earlier, awkward match against a veteran opponent. 'It's not that anyone wants to lose; it's just the concentration. It's only once in a while you can come up to that standard. I don't try to play like that, I try to win, but I don't try to kill myself. That's the big difference, playing big tournaments and just ordinary ones.' He was far too good in the final of Wimbledon for America's exuberant Chuck McKinley, whom he defeated in straight sets, as he would be the following year for his fellow Australian, Martin Mulligan – another straight-sets win.

That was the year of his Grand Slam, the first since

Donald Budge had brought it off in 1938, and Laver pocketed the German and Italian championships into the bargain. He now turned professional, where Rosewall was waiting for him in the National Tennis League.

Laver had youth on his side, and by 1964 had established his superiority, a mark of which was that he won the Wembley Pool pro tournament six years in a row. Rosewall, however, was always lurking in the shadows, and when open tennis was at last brought into being in 1968, it was Rosewall who beat Laver in the final of the French championship.

Perhaps the finest match between them, however, as the professional championships proliferated, took place in Dallas, Texas, in 1972, in the so-called World Championship Tennis finals. Mike Davies, the former British Davis Cup player turned tournaments director, afterwards informed the crowd that it was 'one of the greatest matches in tennis history'.

It might well have been. The tie-break had by now been introduced to put paid to those unending marathons of the past; a controversial move, but one implicit in the growth and dominance of the professional game. Laver, who had been hitting left-handed winners as remarkable as Ken Rosewall's right-handed ones, was in the lead in the fifth set tie-break at 5–4, having averted match point with an ace. Now came two of the finest shots of even 37-year-old Rosewall's career.

He decided that if, as he anticipated, Laver served to his backhand, he would return to Laver's forehand, where he felt he was less likely to put away his volleys. He guessed correctly. As the first serve came hurtling to his backhand, Rosewall managed to strike it back across court. Laver took it on the half-volley, but the ball flew out. Rosewall did better still with the next serve, beating Laver with a glorious passing shot down the sideline. It was now his service, and anti-climax supervened. The serve was a moderate one, and Laver hit it into the net. An exhausted Rosewall forgot even to pocket the cheque he had thus won.

1969 saw Laver bring off his second Grand Slam, and who knows how many more there might have been in between, had he not gone professional. At Wimbledon in 1968 he had little trouble with a fellow Australian left-hander, Tony Roche, whom he beat in the final by 6–3, 6–4, 6–2. In the 1969 final, John Newcombe managed to take the second set 7–5. Tony Roche was again Laver's victim in the final at Forest Hills, with another win in straight sets, Roche taking only five games. Four years later, returning to Australia's Davis Cup team, Laver was still good enough to win all three rubbers against Czechoslovakia in the Inter-Zone final, in the challenge round at Cleveland, Ohio.

Of the tie-break, something should be said. It was first tried at Philadelphia in 1970, with some success. The method was that when the score in a set reached 6–6, twelve points would be played, the first player to gain seven of them winning the set. If after these twelve points the players remained level, the game would go on till one or other achieved a two-point lead. The use of the tie-break in the final set was to be at the discretion of the umpire and varies from country to country.

The I.L.T.F., those King Canutes of tennis, at once vetoed the plan and ordered the American Association to punish its perpetrators. In this they had a stronger case than in their long, perverse opposition to the manifest reality of pro tennis. Now, however, they would crumble very quickly. Five months later, they met and gave permission to national associations to experiment with different forms of tie-break and when, in January 1971, it was made known that the method would be introduced in that year's Wimbledon, the battle was lost and won. There would be no more extraordinary marathons like those between Drobny and Patty, Gonzales and Pasarell; now time, tennis and television – which required the tie-break – waited for no man.

Meanwhile, the women were advancing under the sturdy, sometimes strident leadership of Billie Jean King. Women's Lib was in the air; women all over the West were battling for their rights, and tennis was an obvious target. There was great controversy over whether they were better or worse to watch, whether their restricted physical capacity did not in fact make their game more pleasing, varied and entertaining than the 'slam-bam-thank-you-man' rallies of the males. Unquestionably they got far less money from the game than the men, but Billie Jean and her determined cohorts would change that.

It was in 1970 that Billie Jean, with three Wimbledon and one Forest Hills singles titles behind her, united with seven other female professionals to put on their own tournament in Houston, Texas, snubbing one sanctioned by the U.S.L.T.A. There was inevitably trouble – or rather, more trouble – for the running battle between the U.S.L.T.A. and leading players had by now been going on for over thirty years. The U.S.L.T.A. were authoritarian, the players rebellious.

This time, however, the rebels would generate sufficient leverage to win their cause. They were supported by Mrs Gladys Heldman and the chairman of the Philip Morris tobacco company, who said he would sponsor their tour under the brand name of Virginia Slims. For those of us who feel that cigarettes and sport make uneasy, even absurd bedfellows, there were reservations to express, but there was no doubt that the sponsorship made all the difference. The U.S.L.T.A. was displeased; male tennis players were sceptical. One of them declared that Billie Jean's father had made her a tennis player only to stop her becoming a woman wrestler. The jibe was not only sour but baseless. As we know, Billie Jean had taken up tennis precisely because she saw it as a 'ladylike' sport.

These eight women players subdued their competitive instincts to promote the tour. It was exhausting, but success came very quickly. Soon it became quite clear that they could flourish and prosper without the men. Moreover, 65 per cent of their audiences were male. 'It's not just bird watching,' said the popular Australian player, Judy Tegart Dalton. 'The men can associate their game with our tennis, and they can always sit there and think, "Reckon I could beat that girl."' Gladys Heldman herself admitted, 'There is nothing like a great men's match, but to most people who are not on top of their game, it is more interesting to watch women's tennis, because there is more rallying, and you can actually see the strokes.'

In no time at all, the tournament schedule was increased to twenty-two matches, while the prize money was trebled. In its first full year, 1971, Billie Jean King, who in 1969 had earned $40,000, made more than $100,000, and there was far more to come for all the women pros. 'I'm not money hungry,' she said, 'but I cared about that $100,000 figure, because it was a milestone for women. We're finally appreciated as athletes.'

By 1978 Martina Navratilova, at the age of twenty-one, had won over £100,000, not dollars, in the first *three months* of the year. Even taking account of the fall in the value of money, the progression had been geometrical; as indeed it had been for the money. Being a tennis star had become, in the words of the late Lord (Roy) Thomson, a licence to print money. The sums which had tempted past champions to turn professional seemed utterly negligible in comparison with those now being earned, sometimes, as in the Las Vegas confrontations between champions, in a single match.

For all their progress, the women stars found it hard to win the admiration of the male players. 'I'm just as happy never to see the girls,' remarked Clark Graebner, a leading American player whose wife was also a successful performer in 1972. 'They're not very attractive, and I think it's strange for a wife to be away ...' In 1978, when a group of male tennis players was questioned, the answers were almost uniformly negative. One of them, the American Brian Gottfried, said that if it came to a choice on television between a women's game and an old movie, the movie would have to be very old indeed for him to prefer the tennis.

Inevitably, perhaps, the feminists of the founding generation were a little resentful of the gifted, un-involved girl players who came after them to feast on the fruits of their labour. 'We feel we've done so much for the game,' said the stocky little Rosie Casals – who once exclaimed that she was tired of being known as a relation of the great cellist, and wanted to be known as herself – 'and it hasn't helped our tennis any – battling it out, being suspended, and spending legal fees. Now Chris [Evert] and Evonne [Goolagong] could do a lot for women's tennis, but sometimes they don't seem to care as long as they're not touched by it all and get what they want.'

Such, alas and inevitably, is life, as the self-made parents of coddled children have found so often. Billie Jean King was much more philosophical about it. 'Chris came along without a struggle, but that was the whole point. That's what our tour has been all about.' There was a generosity and a maturity to the words which must surely make those who judged Billie Jean from her surly grimaces on televised tennis think again. Elton John, the rock singer, who at first wrote her off as 'a sour cow', was eventually charmed and fascinated by her, not least by her formidable drive. Twenty years after her first appearance at Wimbledon, she is still capable of giving a fine account of herself, and has run up a record number of titles.

Predictably, given her athleticism and her colossal drive, it did not take long for Billie Jean to put the memory of her unhappy match against Yola Ramirez behind her. The very next year she knocked Margaret Smith out in the second round at Wimbledon. The year after that, the two got to the final, but this time Margaret Smith had much the better of it, winning in straight sets by 6–3, 6–4. Billie Jean had, it was clear, vast potential, but for all the thrust of her serve and volleying, her ground strokes were letting her down.

However, she was bold and dedicated enough, and sufficiently perfectionist, to go to Australia to work on her forehand with the former tennis star, Mervyn

Rose. A new forehand gradually emerged, and in 1966 she won the first of her three consecutive Wimbledon titles. In the 1966 final she beat Maria Bueno, so contrasting a figure and a player, in three sets, losing the second 3–6, as she had won the first, but running away with the final set 6–1. The next year it was Ann Haydon Jones whom she beat in straight sets 6–3, 6–4, as she did Judy Dalton Tegart, though with less ease. Mrs Tegart pushed her surprisingly hard, taking her to sixteen games in the first set, a dozen in the second.

In April 1968 Billie Jean turned pro. Her legs began to give her trouble, and when a car ran into hers, banging her knees against the dashboard, she had to have an operation on her left knee. That was a few months after she had lost to Ann Jones in the 1969 Wimbledon final. Then in the month she lost the 1970 final to Margaret Court, her right knee had to be operated on. The more remarkable that she should have put up such stupendous resistance to Mrs Court in a match which lasted just under two and a half hours, the first set going to twenty-six games, the second to twenty, almost all of them of outstanding quality.

But that was by no means the end of it. Indomitable, Mrs King went on to regain her title in 1972, winning it yet a fifth time in 1973. Curiously, she was much less successful at Forest Hills in the 1960s, winning the singles only in 1967, but in the seventies, her Indian Summer, she took it again in 1972 and 1973. The emerging young lionesses of that era found her a formidable foe.

It was in the seventies that Ken Rosewall twice more reached the Wimbledon final; and twice more

failed to win it. In 1970 his conqueror was his fellow
Australian, John Newcombe, nine years the younger
man at twenty-six, who was so perturbed by the
Centre Court crowd's passionate support for Rosewall
that he said afterwards: 'It was like playing in a
foreign country against a native player. I was asking
myself, why do you hate me? I haven't done anything
against you people.' When Rosewall took the first
set 7–5, the hopes of the spectators rose, only to be
dampened when Newcombe recovered to win the
second 6–3, the third 6–2.

It was in the fourth set, after more than two hours
of play, that the match came dramatically alive. Newcombe was 3–2 ahead and about to serve. Rosewall,
who had just held his service, was sitting on the bottom step of the umpire's chair, plainly exhausted.
'Earlier,' he said, 'I'd found myself waiting for him a
lot, and it drained me of energy and concentration.
He doesn't do it deliberately. It's just the way he
plays. I like to get on with it, but I was conscious that
the longer the match lasted at that pace, the better
he'd be physically. I got a bit tired waiting for him.'

Having, in his gentle way, manifested his displeasure, he rallied astonishingly, a new man. Taking
Newcombe's service to love, the last point being on a
double fault, he held his own service to love into the
bargain. Newcombe served another double fault, his
sixth of the match, dropped his service again, and
Rosewall had, wonder of wonders, taken the set 6–3.
But the little Australian was drained now. There was
a flurry of hope in the fifth game of the final set, when
Rosewall hit a couple of glorious backhand winners
off Newcombe's fierce service, but Newcombe held it
for all that, broke Rosewall's service, and held his

own again for the title, his last shot, appropriately, being a winning forehand volley. This, with his service, had been his chief weapon throughout.

It seemed inconceivable that Rosewall could get to still another final, but in 1974 he did, confronting Jimmy Connors. There was still less doubt about whom the crowd would favour. They had been against Newcombe merely because he was playing their idol, Rosewall, but Connors they were quite prepared to dislike for himself. He was brash, he was noisy, he grunted when he served, and he had a mother-cum-coach who made so much noise in the stands that she had had to be rebuked.

Connors, however, was a young man who could not be intimidated by any crowd. Unlike Newcombe, he found it a spur. 'I realized that the crowd was solidly behind him,' he said. 'Usually, I block the crowd out of my mind, but today it freshened me up. My coach, Pancho Segura, who was watching with my mother, my manager and my fiancée, Chrissy [Evert], played Rosewall many times. His advice was to stay back at the beginning and rally with him to wear him out a bit.' Connors and Evert, by then the outstanding American girl player, were to marry that November – but they did not.

With his steel racket, his physical strength, his double-fisted backhand – on which, Rosewall lamented afterwards, he never seemed able to work – Connors roared away to win in straight sets: 6–1, 6–1, 6–4, the most one-sided final since Hoad annihilated Ashley Cooper in 1957. Poor Rosewall. 'Everything Jimmy touched turned to gold,' he said. 'Certainly he deserved to win, but not by that score.'

Connors' ferocious left-handed service was thrown

into still sharper relief by the weakness of Rosewall's own serve, while the little Australian's forehand was simply not strong enough to trouble the robust young American, whose steel racket commanded the court. 'I just played unbelievable tennis,' he modestly remarked. Connors had followed Chris Evert to the title, and a new era in the game had begun.

The Ups and Downs of Virginia Wade

Virginia Wade, for all her splendid achievements, the titles she took at Forest Hills and, at long last, Wimbledon, has always been a somewhat unlikely tennis player, or rather, tennis professional. As the game became more frenzied, more demanding, more astronomically paid, so this well-educated, well-bred, mettlesome, handsome girl seemed more and more of an anachronism. She was, it is true, as competitive as anybody, more athletic than most, as talented as any. Yet she could, you felt, be doing *something else*. With deference to the Kings, the Everts, the Navratilovas and the Austins, it was hard to imagine them doing anything else that was not merely some other sport. Evert and Austin had been groomed for tennis since childhood. Navratilova was a splendid Amazon from Czechoslovakia who could doubtless have held her own in any athletic field.

Virginia Wade, by contrast, was the daughter of a canon of the Church of England who lived in idyllic retirement in the depths of the English countryside. She had studied mathematics at Sussex University, obtained a degree, and told one at the time that she found the arts people more interesting than the athletes. She seemed, with all her will to win – itself leading to frequent tearful outbursts on the court, far too intelligent, sophisticated and rounded a person to cope with the kind of life of which Sirola and Ann Haydon Jones had complained.

Met for the first time at Hurlingham as an eighteen-year-old in 1964, one was impressed by her lively charm and her intelligence, no less than by the adventurous power of her game. Dark where Christine Truman was fair, smaller and much more mobile than she, Virginia Wade clearly promised to do great things – if she had the time to do them. She wore pigtails then, and her legs would later be admired for their strength at the Cumberland club by no less a footballer than the great Stanley Matthews himself.

Her liking for the grand occasion was already evident. 'I just try to make the fancy shots all the time,' she said, 'so they can't possibly all work. It's a very ambitious game. I feel I can sort of stand at the back of the court and return balls, but not naturally; I get too impatient. But my patience is improving.'

Where Wimbledon, as we have seen, destroyed even Billie Jean King on her first appearances there, Virginia Wade was captivated by it from the start. 'Oh, I enjoy it so much,' she said, 'it's an inspiration. Just the atmosphere and the courts. I play infinitely better with crowded stands than with nobody watching me. It improves my concentration. I sympathize with those people who have tempers because I know just how they feel. It's the matches which aren't important which are the worst. Everybody watching, you don't want to lose your temper; it's when you play right out in the country ...'

Already, tennis was tugging at her, a rival to her studies at Sussex. 'Tennis,' she said, 'is such a temptation, it's just not true.'

Technically she was and is a British player, but
one wonders how good she would have become had
her father not been sent to South Africa. While he
was Archdeacon of Durban, she learned the game,
returning permanently to England only when she was
fifteen years old.

The romance between the British tennis public
and 'Ginny' was of a different kind from that with
Christine Truman. With Ann Haydon Jones, it can
scarcely be said that there was a romance at all. Compact, muscular, ironic, she did not invite the sympathy extended to Christine Truman, who was always
marginally too good to be true, yet never quite good
enough. Nor did she, in her consistent way, plunge
so often from the peaks to the trough, as did Virginia
Wade, a roller-coaster of a player, perpetually raising
expectations which her temperament prevented her
from gratifying.

She duly took her degree at Sussex in maths and
physics in 1966, playing in the Wightman Cup the
while. In this competition, as elsewhere, she was tantalizingly unpredictable. In 1968, her first great year
and the one in which she took the American title, she
helped Britain to win it. Two years later, she lost the
key rubber in the doubles.

Having put her thousands of admirers through
hoops for years – as she subsequently would for years
more – Virginia Wade surpassed herself in 1968, with
a magnificent victory in the first open tournament at
Forest Hills. When she had won, she stood on a ros-
trum in the centre of the stadium with Herman David,
President of the All England Club, whose courageous,
honest policies had done so much the year before to
destroy shamateurism. One might add that had it

been left to Mr David, Bunny Austin by then would
have been restored to membership of the club.

In the final, Virginia Wade beat none other than
Billie Jean King, and did so in a couple of sets in
forty-one minutes. Throughout the tournament she
had played splendid tennis. That her best was probably the best in the world had never been in much
doubt; that she could produce it consistently, even in
one match, let alone over a tournament, had been altogether another matter.

Losing a set in the first round against the seventh-
ranked American girl, she would drop no more. Mrs
King gave her a rather better match than the score
suggests. She had two break points against Miss Wade
in the sixth game of the first set, but Virginia saved
them, characteristically, first with a winning service,
then with a smash. Breaking service herself with a well-
placed lob, she then held her own service with ease
for the first set. In the second, she broke Billie Jean's
service in the very first game, and after that Billie
Jean was always struggling to stay in the match.

In the last two games, Billie Jean managed but one
point. Breaking service to take her lead to 5–2,
Virginia took the last point with one of her most
ferocious forehands, then held her own service again
to run out at 6–4, 6–2.

That should have been the start of something good,
if not extraordinary, but it was not. Wimbledon,
which was clearly next in Virginia's sights, and would
please her still more than her success at Forest Hills,
would continue to elude her for another whole decade.

The most memorable game of her progress to the
1977 Wimbledon championship was her semi-final

against Chris Evert, the alleged 'Ice Maiden' and favourite for the tournament, whom she beat in an enthralling match. The final itself, against the huge Dutch girl, Betty Stove, was the sheerest anti-climax. Nerves overtook not only Virginia Wade, who after all had the pressure of the expectations of the Centre Court crowd and millions of invisible Britons to cope with, but on Betty Stove too, remotest of outsiders.

It was said at the time that during the semi-final Miss Evert's gaze kept drifting mournfully towards the competitors' seats, looking in vain for her former fiancé, Jimmy Connors, who had promised to come to watch her, but never did. Perhaps it was so. Perhaps her disappointment – she seemed still plainly in love with him – had something to do with her defeat, but there was no taking the credit away from Virginia Wade and her excellence.

In the previous year's semi-final, Evonne Cawley (née Goolagong), the pretty, athletic Aboriginal girl, had annihilated her 6–1, 6–2. Memories of that display were momentarily laid to rest by her performance against Chris Evert, but revived by the ineptitude of the final. Against Mrs Cawley, Virginia's backhand had gone utterly to pieces. Against Miss Evert, in 1977, it was thoroughly effective, as was everything else in her game. Against Miss Stove, anything was likely to go wrong at any time, but fortunately for Miss Wade, her erratic play was complemented by Miss Stove's own.

The final winning score – greeted by the crowd with a roar of what was surely relief as much as triumph – was 4–6, 6–3, 6–1. Could it happen again, the spectators must have asked themselves with horror, as the first set slipped out of Miss Wade's grasp? Was this, the very final, going to be one more occasion on which their heroine would flatter to deceive? The match had even begun with Betty Stove taking a point off Virginia's serve with a lob – no good augury. When Miss Stove went into the lead at 5–4, it was with a love game off Virginia's potentially devastating serve; two errors by Miss Wade, two winners from Miss Stove. There was a comedy of errors even in the final game of the set, where Miss Wade had a point for five-all, and Miss Stove double-faulted, but she held on.

In the second set it seemed that Virginia had taken hold of herself and her game at last. She ran quickly into a 3–0 lead, only to lose three games in a row, then win the next three. In the final set Miss Stove seemed to have given up the ghost. She went 4–0 down, retrieved a game, but lost the next two. The first match point went begging, the second Virginia won with a forehand off Miss Stove's service, which provoked a volley into the net. Miss Stove took defeat with characteristic good grace, one of those players who seem essentially supporting cast, but can beat any star on an off day.

It had been a traumatically difficult year for Virginia Wade. Above all, she had been working as hard and painfully to remodel her serve as some golfers have to work to remodel their swing. It was said of her, as though this were something positive and laudable, that she had become enormously more professional, but for some of us her allure had lain in the very fact that however good she was, she was much more than a professional – an amateur in the old, true sense of the word; one with infinitely broader horizons than those whose life is limited by sport. On them, surely, Orlando Sirola had the last word.

She was now, together with Billie Jean King, a

member of the World Team Tennis's New York
Apples, a very different world from the genteel re-
finement of Wimbledon. World Team Tennis scorned
to submit the fans to the subtleties of traditional
scoring; games would end with such scores as 24–28.
In Madison Square Garden, not long after she had
won Wimbledon, Virginia Wade found herself con-
fronted with a fat New York taxi driver who had
won, by ballot, the right to confront her on the court,
but could scarcely get the ball over the net. Cheer-
leaders shrieked and danced their way on to the
court. 'It pays the bills,' said Virginia Wade.

She had, at twenty-three, won Forest Hills without
being 'professional', and she had permitted herself
such splendid observations as, 'I'm not equipped
mentally to play week after week; I should never play
more than three weeks on the trot because I get stale
so quickly,' and, 'I hate people who work too hard. I
I think laziness is the absolute end, but it is overwork
that I really despise.' Here was the old English attitude, implicit in which was a sense of proportion
which kept sport, by definition, in its place. The
trouble with nature's true amateurs is that when they
are drawn into the professional sporting world they
are worn down by that world. They are never likely
to bring it up to their own level. The contemporary
world of professional tennis, alas, presents itself to the
outsider as one of greedy, spoiled children, pocketing
sums of money out of all proportion to their calling –
though who, after all, is to set the criteria? Virginia
Wade, though she pertinently complained that English
students are pushed too early into specialized studies
and that she did not enjoy the maths and physics she
learned at Sussex University, was not of that ilk.

Her service, once thought of as the best any woman in the game possessed, somehow fell apart in 1976. There was not much time to put it together before Wimbledon. She had begun trying to improve it the previous December with the coach, Ham Richardson, himself once an elegant player. He said it 'nearly killed him' to see her wasting so much energy. Progress was made, but not enough; she tried another coach, Jerry Teeguarden, having twice lost badly to the little blonde Devon girl, Sue Barker. Now, a compromise was worked out. It was a better service, though scarcely better than the one she had had before it fell mysteriously to pieces. It stuttered when she played at Eastbourne, but then she went home to Kent and hit nearly seventy serves on the family tennis court, until she felt that she had got it right.

What she did seem to have acquired among the pros (it would be less evident after 1977) was greater calm. A more versatile player than the relentless, baselining Chris Evert, she weathered an awkward spell in that semi-final. 'The old Ginny,' said a player, 'would have gone on until the blood vessels were sticking out of her forehead, and she would have blown four games in the meantime. The new Virginia went and sat on the grass by the umpire's chair, and relaxed her neck and back muscles. She sees the signs now. It's the same car, but it's being driven by a different person.'

By 1978 that powerful, beautifully streamlined car was displaying its old faults of eccentricity, labouring to leave behind vehicles far inferior to itself. Still, Virginia Wade had won both Forest Hills and Wimbledon. What other English girl could say as much?

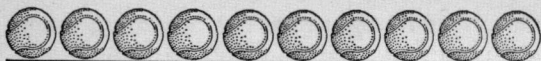

The Game Grows Harsher

When Stan Smith won an epic Wimbledon final against Ilie Nastase in 1972, there were elements about it of a morality play. That the field had been severely enfeebled by another row between the tennis establishment and the pros was almost irrelevant. Two very fine players reached the final, and a very fine final they played. But Nastase, the darling of the teenage girls with his sultry good looks, his gipsy elegance and his lank black hair, was perfectly cast as the Bad Guy against the tall, blond, balding Stan Smith's Good Guy.

Nastase on court could be a holy terror, a monster of gamesmanship, a baiter of umpires, a perpetrator of weak, self-indulgent jokes which enraptured the sycophantic gallery, but sickened the more objective; a rotten loser and an overgrown adolescent. Clark Graebner, the American, once became so exasperated by him at the Albert Hall that he jumped the net and threatened to punch him, whereupon Nastase behaved.

Smith, by utter contrast, was a player who could certainly overawe his opponents with his physical and mental presence, but one who would never stoop to the cheap stratagems of Nastase. It was all very well for people who knew Nastase to tell us that off court he was the kindest, gentlest, most sensitive man; we could only go by what happened when he was on it – by such incidents as his monumental row with the tournament referee one year at Bournemouth ('You call me *Mr* Nastase'), by his behaviour in the game against John McEnroe in the 1979 American championships, and by his still worse behaviour the following January in the Braniff Doubles at Earls Court.

It remained equally true that Nastase, a Rumanian and a protégé of his compatriot Ion Tiriac, a huge buccaneer of a player, was at his best perhaps the most delightfully accomplished player of his day. There seemed nothing he could not do, no stroke he could not elegantly and powerfully make. His touch was delightful, his imaginative strategy a joy. He could wallop a serve or a smash with the best of them, yet bring off as delicate a shot as a Lenglen or an Austin. Temperament was his trouble. For all the opponents he upset, the final victim was himself. He should, given his superior powers, have beaten Smith, but did not. Then came the Borgs, the Connors and the McEnroes, and he was swept away.

You might properly call him a Latin player, even if the Rumanians' claim to be Latins has not always fallen on sympathetic ears. He had the touch, the flair and the disposition; though as Spain's Manuel Santana (Wimbledon's champion in 1966, Forest Hills' in 1965) and Manuel Orantes (Forest Hills winner in 1975) both showed, that explosive temperament was not an essential ingredient. Santana, a player of exquisite control and splendid reflexes, was admirably good-natured. Orantes, once a ball boy, son of a lens grinder, overcame wretched luck with injuries for his success.

Born in Bucharest in 1946, an 11 lb baby, and

brought up fifty yards from the principal tennis stadium, Nastase's first love was soccer, though he took up tennis at seven and began to play in tournaments when he was twelve. Ken Rosewall was his idol. When he first came to play him, he could never beat him. 'I could never understand,' he said, 'how he could hit shots like he does, how he was so quick, how he was always in position. I liked his game so much I wanted to clap when he passed me.' Rosewall – who had crashed to Jimmy Connors in the 1974 Forest Hills final even more cataclysmically than a few months earlier at Wimbledon – actually beat Nastase in November 1977 in the three-set final of the Gunze Tournament in Tokyo, though giving away thirteen years.

Nastase's brother, Constantini, a Rumanian Davis Cup player, was also thirteen years his senior; his success, his travel beyond the frontiers of that beleaguered Iron Curtain country, were clearly a stimulus to Ilie. An understanding coach called Colonel Chivaru, who said he had to do little more than put a racket in Ilie's hand, weaned him gradually away from soccer. 'I like,' Chivaru said, 'players who use a lot of wrist.' He 'never had to change his strokes'. As a competitor, the greatest influence on Nastase was Tiriac, whom he watched with awe, battling on the ice hockey rink.

Nastase's final with Stan Smith redeemed a 1972 Wimbledon which till then had largely been dull. It lasted five sets and two hours forty-five minutes, Nastase picking up the first and fourth set by 6–4. Not since 1963, astonishingly enough, had an American won at Wimbledon and Nastase, who had played through the tournament in an uncharacteristically relaxed mood, convinced despite his number two seed-ing that he had no chance, seemed likely to maintain that sequence. 'I play like in practice,' he observed. 'I hit shots you only hit when you don't care.'

He certainly cared about the final, but temperament and his topspin cross-court forehand let him down. Nastase elected to believe it was his racket; he was perpetually and alternately banging and plucking its strings. Smith contrived to miss no fewer than eleven backhands in that first set, but Nastase was too deep in his own misery. He emerged from it sufficiently to win the first set by 6–4, and now seemed at peace with his racket. Though he had not the reach and power of Smith, he had much greater speed, and a far greater capacity for surprise.

Since Smith's usually fearsome service was curiously lacking in force, Nastase, essentially a clay-court player, seemed on to a good thing. Appearances were deceptive. Even though Nastase promptly broke Smith's wavering service in the first game of the second set, he served a weirdly distracted game himself, losing to love as Smith had just done.

This reprieve was of great psychological value to Smith, who began dominating the net in something of his usual commanding style, even if his service was still not at its best. He won this set and the next, quickly broke 'Nasty's' service in the fourth, and seemed well on his way to the title. Nastase, endlessly unpredictable, however, now woke up, moved about the court with impressive speed, and drew level at 4–4. Breaking Smith's service, he went into the lead; holding his own, he won the set. Two sets all. It was the first Sunday final in the history of Wimbledon – Saturday had been rained out – and the match was now rising to meet the unique occasion.

The fifth game was probably decisive. Smith was forty–love ahead when Nastase dropped a spinning lob on his baseline, got back to deuce, and three times had advantage point for a break. Smith saved every one of them, the last with a fulminating serve, and rounded off the game with a drop shot straight out of Nastase's book.

He now seemed to have fathomed Nastase's service, though he was helped in the ninth game by a fluky drop shot off the wood of his racket. Now Smith was in the driver's seat. Nastase saved two match points, but he was clearly struggling. A poor shot off a high backhand gave the title to Smith.

By September the pros had composed their quarrel with the establishment, and it was a full field which competed at Forest Hills. The employment of the tie-break, which many leading players detested as an arbitrary short-cut, and the wretched state of the grass combined to make the tournament something of a lottery. Nevertheless, Nastase's achievement in winning the title against the gifted black player Arthur Ashe – who would soon emulate Althea Gibson by winning Wimbledon – was a superb one.

This match, too, went to five sets, Nastase losing the third of them on the controversial tie-break, and the first set 3–6. He thus became the third 'Latinate', or, if you prefer it, 'touch player', to win the title since the war, following in the steps of Santana and the elegant Rafael Osuna of Mexico; Orantes was to come.

Ashe had beaten Stan Smith on the way but although Nastase had had a much easier passage, his performance in a fluctuating, dramatic final made him a proper champion. Again, there was to be an intriguing contrast of styles, the volatile Nastase against the calm, contained, almost cerebral Ashe. The tension was manifest from the first game when Ashe twice double-faulted and lost his serve, then Nastase lost his in turn. A break of service in the eighth game eventually put Ashe in a position to hold his own serve and take the set.

Nastase then took wing, winning the second set 6–3, but a dubious call destroyed his concentration and he lost his temper. When another doubtful call was made in the tie-breaker, he threw a towel and hit a ball at the linesman. Not unexpectedly in the circumstances, the more composed Ashe won the tie-breaker 5–1.

There was every sign in the first half-dozen games of the next set that it would continue to be Ashe. With Nastase losing his service and Ashe scoring aces off his, the black American ran into a 4–2 lead. But it has always been dangerous to write off Nastase. As the evening wore on, so Ashe seemed to feel the virtue go out of him. His service flagged, and his always doubtful forehand volley faltered, too. Nastase began to hit winning topspin forehands down the line, pulled back to four-all, and won the next two games into the bargain for the set.

Again it seemed that Ashe would take over when he promptly broke Nastase's service in the first game of the final set, but Nastase broke back immediately, and ran into the kind of form which Ashe could never match. He broke through again for 4–2, then ran out the winner at 6–3; the first and so far the only Rumanian to have won the United States title.

Nastase has had a curious love–hate relationship with another maverick of the tennis courts, Jimmy

Connors, the young American left-hander who annihilated Rosewall in those two 1974 finals, snubbed the
Duke and Duchess of Kent by practising on an outside court instead of attending the Wimbledon parade
of champions in 1977, and has generally been at the
eye of the hurricane throughout his career.

Connors, who comes from St Louis, clearly felt at
one stage that he was getting too close to Nastase, with
unfortunate consequences whenever they met on the
tennis court. This alone could explain, if it hardly
excused, what he said to Nastase in Puerto Rico a
couple of months after his gauche behaviour at Wimbledon.

The two were there to play a head-to-head match
for a vast sum of money, promoted by Connors's
original mentor and subsequent adversary in law, Bill
Riordan. News was just beginning to come through
of a catastrophic earthquake in Bucharest, but it had
carefully been kept from Nastase. When Connors
arrived on the practice courts of the Cerro Mar Hotel,
however, he greeted Nastase, 'Hey, buddy, you'd
better call Bucharest. You might not have a house any
more.' Fortunately, Nastase took it as merely the ex-
tension of a long-running joke between them. 'I had
no idea what he really meant,' he would say. In the
event Connors, who would certainly have been ideal
casting for the younger Mickey Rooney in a 'bio-pic',
won the confrontation.

Connors, like Nastase, has had his apologists, not
least after the Wimbledon contretemps, but not even
the most fervent of them could pretend he was distinguished by his charm. There have been, it is true,
moments of chivalry, not least at a major tournament
in Madison Square Garden early in 1980, when he

refused to accept a point which he felt had been wrongly given him.

It might fairly be said that Connors was the product of that well-known American phenomenon, 'Mom-ism'. One hears nothing in his odyssey about his father, merely about his mother and grandmother, those two formidable tennis-playing, tennis-coaching women who had him playing from infancy, tied his left hand behind his back to make sure he really was a left-hander, and inspired him with that burning wish to take on and take it out of the world which was one of the secrets of his triumphs. Mom was Gloria Connors, grandmother was 'Two Mom'. At the worst moments of his defeat by Arthur Ashe in the 1975 Wimbledon singles with the Centre Court crowd baying for his doom, he pulled out of his sock a crumpled letter from Two Mom, written years before, telling him to give his all.

After Mom and Two Mom came the two Panchos, Segura and Gonzales, and after them came the icono-clastic Riordan, eternally fighting the tennis establish-ment – this time the professional one – involving Connors in his lawsuits, encouraging him to be ob-streperous, yet taking him, when he believed him too big for his boots, around a children's cancer ward in New York.

Two Mom would tell him to 'pull up his socks' – those very socks in which he stowed her letter – 'and just be better than everybody else'. He was, he knew, 'from Belleville, the wrong side of the river, and the important tennis was being played in the country clubs on the other side in St Louis. I wasn't their kind, but I had to play there, and Two Mom and Mom impressed on me that people might not like me, but it was okay; we'd do it our way, and show them.'

Show them they did. Connors's strength, for all his muscularity, was never the 'big' serve, or the walloping volley, but rather his speed around the court, his exceptional eye, his smoothly measured ground strokes, and his capacity to hit the ball early, precisely and with force. No one, it was said, had taken the ball quite so early since Lew Hoad. It has been an unusual and intriguing feature of the modern game that Connors and Borg, two of its outstanding practitioners, should not be serve-and-volley men. Pancho Gonzales, indeed, has not been the only one to describe Borg as 'a baseliner'.

At sixteen, Connors was sent by Mom and Two Mom to Los Angeles to study under Segura and Gonzales; chiefly the little Ecuadorian, Segura. 'My mother and grandmother,' Connors has said, 'had already given me all the strokes. I went to Pancho as a tennis player. What he did was mainly to teach me the mental outlook to the game.'

He would sit for hours talking with the Panchos – a willing perfectionist. 'How can it not rub off on you – two of the greatest players, two of the greatest guys of all time?' For a player who has been denounced for his conceit Connors, in these important early years, displayed substantial humility. What he remained was an outsider. When Arthur Ashe, whom Connors was suing at the time in one of the lawsuits inspired by Riordan, beat him at Wimbledon he said, 'Connors has paid a dear price for letting Riordan manoeuvre him. In effect, Connors has traded in his soul. He is nearly friendless among the players. He offends the public with vulgarity and foul language ... Somehow I feel that Jimmy set out to fill some role that had been created for him, but that along the way he forgot where acting took over from reality. He has fulfilled the image and made a villain of himself, and that is a sad thing for a 22-year-old boy. Worse, he seems to revel in it.'

Others, again, felt Connors needed this kind of animosity to make him an effective player; as he seemed, indeed, to feel himself, at the time of his breach with Nastase. Chris Evert, during their several engagements, seemed to do something to domesticate him. She described him as gentle, though she was not in the end gently put aside. When he did recapture his soul, or at least his independence from Riordan, and loosen his ties with his mother, redemption – or help – came from an unlikely quarter. Marjorie Wallace, the Miss World of that time, had led a hectic, highly publicized life, yet she seemed to be a liberating influence on Connors. 'Nowadays,' wrote an English journalist at the time of the 1976 Wimbledon, 'scarcely a Connors sentence seems to go by without a mention of Marjorie Wallace.'

Unfortunately for Connors, who made his peace even with the American Davis Cup team and its captain, the former tennis star Dennis Ralston, this was the time of the emergence of Borg; and after Borg would come McEnroe.

At first, though not for very long, Connors had the edge on Borg, and even when it was plain that the balance had shifted, he was able to beat him a second time in the final at Forest Hills, though primarily because Borg had a badly blistered thumb, and would probably not have played at all had it not been for the anguished demands of television.

After Borg had defeated Connors in a fluctuating,

unpredictable 1977 Wimbledon final, he remarked, 'Connors beat me seven times out of the previous nine meetings because, before, he was mentally tough to play against, always hitting hard with good depth. But he doesn't scare me any more.'

Scare him or not, Connors had been good enough to beat him in the final at Forest Hills two years earlier, winning by three sets to one, the third set being decided on a tie-break. Gradually Connors managed to cope with Borg's formidable topspin forehand, a shot he had conceived and copied from the table tennis loop shot, and which caused the ball frequently to bounce up to shoulder height. The 1978 Wimbledon final, in which the two met again, showed Borg utterly superior, winning in straight sets against a Connors who simply could not live with him. Whereas in 1977 Borg, 4–0 up in the fifth set, had been pegged back to 4–4, then accelerated to win, now he dominated Connors, winning by 6–2, 6–2, 6–3.

Connors, who three years ago had been making such sums as half a million dollars for beating John Newcombe at Caesar's Palace, swore, 'I'll follow Borg to the ends of the earth. I'll stay with the so-and-so until I beat him.' This, as we know, he did soon afterwards at Forest Hills, though the victory, however sweet to him, was a pretty hollow one. You might even have called it a victory for television.

Having introduced Borg into our story, it is high time to give chapter and verse on him; the player who first equalled then surpassed Fred Perry's record at Wimbledon and has dominated the game in a way that seemed impossible in modern times. He reasserted the importance and the validity of ground strokes, and it has been said of him that such is his concentration that you could fire off a cannon behind him and it would make no difference.

It is not easy to reconcile this picture of Borg with the figure one sees on court, festooned with commercial insignia, long blond hair secured by a headband advertising one thing, sweatbands advertising something else; a figure given to a strange, almost obsessive ritual, as he awaits service. Nervously – or so it seems – he shifts from one foot to the other, raising his hand half-way, sometimes all the way, to his mouth. The incantation, by and large, seems to work, though his own thundering service works even better. He is at once exceedingly fast and not a bit graceful; he rolls and lumbers about the court. He has been the darling of teenage girls, yet his eyes are close-set, he has a straggle of beard, his aura is almost morose. Perpetual use of his celebrated topspin forehand, kicking up to trouble his opponents, has led to a distorting growth of muscle beneath his right shoulder blades, just as Rod Laver's freckled left forearm was thickened by perpetual use of his topspin backhand. Borg's backhand is double-fisted and formidable.

Borg sees himself not as 'Iceborg', his nickname among the pros, but as a player who has won the battle with himself: unlikeliest of victories among today's tennis stars. 'I am not as cool as everybody thinks,' he has said. 'Sometimes on court I have a lot of emotion inside, but I don't show it. I get very nervous, like anybody else. When I started to play tennis, I had a very bad temper. I was one of the worst in my club in my home town.'

His home town was Sodertlage, near Stockholm, where he was born on 6 June 1956. To a naturally powerful build, a splendid eye and superb reflexes was added the advantage of an abnormally low pulse rate, a mere 35. His first love was ice hockey, but at the age of nine his father, a salesman, won a tennis racket in a table tennis tournament, and gave it to Borg. At once Bjorn began to hit balls against the garage wall. Graduation to the tennis courts which stood, providentially, only a hundred yards away was almost as swift. Concurrently he still played ice hockey, but gave it and all other sports up at the age of thirteen for the curious but perhaps significant reason that he had won nothing much in ice hockey, but two junior tournaments in tennis, 'And I knew that tennis would offer the greatest rewards.' Indeed it did. When, at the age of fifteen, he was urgently seeking permission to leave school and concentrate on tennis, he swore he would make a million dollars by the time he was twenty. The promise was abundantly fulfilled. In 1977 alone, the year of his second success at Wimbledon, he was estimated to have earned £600,000; in 1978 about a million pounds, £85,000 of it in prize money in the first two months of the year; in 1979 and 1980 still more: over $3 million per year. His rackets came from the manufacturer Donnay, his clothes from Fila leisure wear, his headband from Tuborg, and his wristbands from the airline S.A.S. – a living, breathing, walking, tennis-playing advertisement.

Borg is a frugal young man, given to staying in hotels eschewed by players making only a fraction of his millions, but he has admitted that there was a time early in his precocious career when he was doing too much, too fast. His parents – whom he moved to Monte Carlo, where he himself had moved to escape

Sweden's punitive income tax – urged him to relax. So did Lennart Bergelin, his coach and confidant, once an excellent Davis Cup man himself. 'When you are very young,' Borg has confessed, 'you can think only of winning more and more tournaments and getting more and more money. It's fun, it's novelty, it makes you feel important. It's no good people coming to you to straighten you out. No matter how much you love or respect them, you tell yourself that you know what you want to do. You know yourself better than anyone. So you say, "Okay, I'll think about it," but you know deep down you will do what you want. If you think you can win everything with no bad effects, you will go for it. You have no reason to be pessimistic. You are on a sort of trip.

'Well, one day I suddenly saw their point of view. It wasn't their persuasion; it came from inside me. I thought, "I'm doing too much. The pleasure is going from it. There's not much fun any more."' So he withdrew from a £280,000 contract for team tennis with Cleveland. 'Surely,' he observed philosophically, 'you must reach a point when you realize that money can only buy you certain things in life. A man needs only one house, one car, he can wear only one set of clothes at a time.'

Borg was three days away from his eighteenth birthday when he won his first international title, beating Ilie Nastase in straight sets at the Foro Italico in Rome to become the Italian champion. Two years later it would be Nastase whom he would beat to win his first Wimbledon final. The previous month he had reached the vastly lucrative finals of the World Championship Tennis circuit, in Dallas. His first two matches were broadcast on Swedish radio, and heard by an estimated four million listeners out of a population of seven million. Borg reached the final and took the powerful Australian, John Newcombe, to four sets.

Though beaten in Rome, Nastase, self-destructive and wayward, yet in his day invincible, would continue for a time to give Borg trouble.

In the Masters championship of 1975, held in, of all places, Borg's own Stockholm, Nastase beat him in the final in straight sets. On his way there, Nastase had succeeded in provoking to fury even the mild and cultivated Arthur Ashe. Curiously, Ashe himself was not the target of Nastase's antics. A heckler in the crowd had taunted him each time he bounced the ball before he served. Nastase, who finds it hard to rise above such things, had shouted back. The umpire warned Nastase to keep playing, but Nastase kept stopping to reply to the heckler and Ashe eventually stalked off the court, incensed, before the referee could disqualify Nastase. After a double disqualification by the referee, Ashe was reinstated and Nastase said it with flowers; made a timid, generous apology to him, accompanied by a large bouquet. 'That was so typical of Nastase,' said Ashe, always a generous man himself. 'You can't be mad at the guy for long.'

For Nastase, his behaviour seemed to have had a curiously calming, beneficial effect. He advanced to the semi-finals in which he played glorious tennis to defeat the fine left-handed Argentinian, Guillermo Vilas, 6–0, 6–3, 6–4. Then it was the final with Borg, who had beaten Ashe. From this match you could never have predicted the young Swede's future domination of world tennis, let alone his easy conquest of Nastase at Wimbledon in the final the following year.

Nastase was almost unplayable, serving magnificently, routing Borg with his delicate but strong volleys and his subtle lobs. He took the match in straight sets, 6–2, 6–2, 6–1.

What, then, had happened between Stockholm and Wimbledon? The second tournament was, of course, on grass, to whose lower bounce Borg was steadily adjusting; but then Nastase was also well used to Wimbledon by now. Besides, he had been playing wonderfully well, reaching the final – like Borg himself – without dropping a set, and thrashing Charlie Pasarell in the quarter-finals with a brilliant performance.

When Nastase took a 3–0 lead in the first set and had three points to break service for 4–0, it seemed that Borg would go the way he had in Stockholm less than a year before. Then something went wrong. In the words of Nastase's biographer, Richard Evans, 'You couldn't have electrocuted a fly with the amount of energy he was giving off that day.' Had he behaved too well, too long? Had the mental strength he needed to repress his natural volatility now failed him when he needed it to win?

Whatever the explanation, Borg, much less graceful but exceedingly fast, made light even of a painful stomach muscle which he had to spray at each change-over. Where Nastase was untypically passive, he was selectively aggressive, hitting the ball harder and longer, scoring with his deep, accurate, strong service. He took the first set 6–4, the second 6–2, and though Nastase belatedly came to life in the third, it was too late. He allowed Borg to break his service at 7–7, and lost the last game to love.

The 1977 centenary final at Wimbledon was a

vastly different affair. To the joy of the royalist Centre Court spectators, Borg beat Connors, who had snubbed the Duke and Duchess of Kent, but it was an extremely close-run thing. 'If two guys are the best in the world,' said Connors afterwards, in his earthy way, 'every time they go out they are at each other's throats all the time. I'm in there fighting my butt off, and he's doing the same. There's no riding out hot streaks, and no waiting for the cold streaks to end. You just stay in there and hope, and if that's not good enough, then you're finished. I was down four games [in the final set] but I got back to 4–4, and the match could have been mine very easily.'

So it could. In a match which began with both men bombarding one another from the baseline, Connors was at first the sharper, hitting his forehands to a better length, coming swiftly to the net, playing his best tennis of the tournament. The first set was his, and as Borg said afterwards, 'If he'd broken my service in the second set and won it and led by two sets to love, then I think there was no way I could have won.'

It was, in the third game of that set, a very near thing, but Borg held on, steadied, began hitting irresistible passing shots, broke Connors's service three times, another three in the third set, but faltered again in the fourth. Untypical breaks in his concentration lost him his service in the sixth game, and though he broke back immediately in a game which produced the best rally in the match – a thing of astonishing reflexes and reversals by the net – Connors won at 7–5. Borg's double fault helped Connors to break service in the vital game, and the match was still largely a thing of baseline rallies.

In the last set Borg roared away into a 4-0 lead, breaking Connors's service at once, and holding his own with the help of a spectacular half-volley on the forehand which flew all the way from the baseline to pass Connors at breathtaking speed. Another service break, featuring a majestic backhand down the line, a further win off his own service, and all seemed over.

Not a bit of it. Connors, who has confessed that he 'hates' tennis balls, just as Borg has said he loves them, took the fifth game with the help of a net cord, and bravely fought his way back to 4-4. Fortune seemed with him; another net cord helped him in the eighth game.

It did not last. Borg now raised his game to a level where Connors, who had clearly given his all, could not follow him. The last two games were his, and with them his second title.

1978 was quite another story. Though Borg began uncertainly, dropping the first two games and having trouble with his topspin backhand, he then got quickly into gear, exploited Connors's penchant for double faults, hit winners off his own service, and ran out at 6-2, 6-2, 6-3. The topspin forehand he had learned at table tennis had seldom been so lethally effective.

In 1979 he won Wimbledon for the fourth time in a row, mastering the cyclonic serving of tall Roscoe Tanner in the final. When he met Tanner again, however, in the quarter-final of the U.S. championships, he lost, and the Grand Slam had passed him by again.

Those four Wimbledons, however, were substantial consolation. At a time when tennis had become so highly professionalized, when its prizes had become almost indecently huge, and when the various Masters and World championships had proliferated to the point of confusion, Wimbledon still meant most to Borg. It was, he said, 'the most important thing of all. The money is much bigger in other places, but nothing can even compare to Wimbledon. It's tradition, it's everything, and when you play there, you really, really don't care if you make even one dollar; that's the truth.' Just before he won his third title, he said, 'I still feel that way, absolutely. Wimbledon is always going to be my biggest ambition. I don't mind to win it ten times.'

Outside tennis his existence seems peripheral. He has kept closely to his family, to his coach Bergelin, whom he reputedly looks on as an older brother, and to the Rumanian tennis girl, Mariana Simonescu, who, he said, had made him happy. 'When I am not playing tennis, I am usually too tired to do anything else. Sometimes I want to sleep for one week. I enjoy sleeping, you know. I just enjoy being in my own house. In Monte Carlo there is no problem about getting away from people. It is such a small place, but there are a lot of famous people there so no one bothers you.'

Tactically, Borg and Bergelin leave nothing to chance, just as they worked away on Borg's service until it had matched the rest of his formidable game. When he beat Connors so easily at Wimbledon in 1978, it had been decided that they would use 'a plan that involved slicing backhands on to his forehand and going in. My intention was to serve hard, and to attack his weaker second serve. It worked because the court was soft and the ball kept low.'

Even now, Borg is neither invincible nor invulnerable, though as Fred Perry has said, 'When people play Borg now they are beaten before they go on

court.' Curiously, he was not ranked number one
in the world until 1977, and then it was only for a
week, after which he had to wait till April 1979
to displace Connors for only the second time in five
years. That, however, may have more to say about
computers than it does about Borg. A little odd that
a man who has been compared with a machine should
be slighted by a real one.

Goolagong, Evert and Navratilova

Billie Jean and her cohorts were followed by Evonne Goolagong, Chris Evert and Martina Navratilova – an Australian Aborigine, a composed American, and a flamboyant Czech defector.

Evonne Goolagong's story was almost too good to be true; it is strange that no one yet has made a film about it. Born into an Aborigine family in the country town of Barellan, she was spotted as a child by a colleague of the Sydney tennis coach Vic Edwards, who, like some modern Pygmalion, whisked her away to Sydney. There he coached her, gave her, after the manner of Shaw's Henry Higgins, elocution lessons, dedicated her life to tennis, and helped her turn into a notable champion.

What Evonne Goolagong felt about this we are unlikely ever to know. There has always been a shy reserve about her. She has always refused to be drawn into any kind of statement or stand about her race. She won championships with a kind of distracted brilliance. For years she seemed to submit to the abrasive management of Edwards. Then suddenly, in 1975, she married the British tennis player Roger Cawley, oblivious of Edwards's displeasure, and parted from him as abruptly as he himself had wrenched her out of her own background.

A player with a fine, lithe physique, flowing movement and an exceptional backhand, she was utterly different from all her women contemporaries, whether they were as strident as Billie Jean King, bland as Chrissie Evert, or assertive as Navratilova. Her transistor radio perpetually tuned to pop music, her conversation turned blithely to fashion or dancing but seldom tennis, she seemed to glide through life; though it must certainly have been very lonely for her when she first made the American tour. No one would ever say a word against her; what was there to say? Even Billie Jean King called her 'a beboppy teenager type who's a lovely person', while her fellow Australian, Judy Tegart, mumbled that she was 'a typical Aborigine; and I don't mean that in a racial sense, but in the "she's all right, mate" sense'. Whatever that meant.

Nobody much liked Edwards, whose demands – payment for interviews with his protégée, payment for television appearances connected with her tournaments – endeared him very little. He it was who said patronizingly that she had a tendency to 'go walkabout' in the aboriginal way, to let her mind simply wander from the business, or the tennis, in hand. When Teddy Tinling, the tall, bald tennis dress designer, said in 1977 that he was no longer going to dress Evonne, she was an 'anachronism', the gratuitous silliness of his remark would scarcely have bothered her. Besides, if she was an anachronism, one felt, then the sooner the clock of women's tennis could be turned back, the better.

She first came to Europe at nineteen, captivated everybody, and won the Wimbledon title the following year, beating that utterly contrasting Australian, Margaret Court, in the final. Mrs Court remarked

afterwards, somewhat presumptuously, that she was
'... concerned about Evonne's state of mind; now
that she has won Wimbledon so young, she may feel
she has nothing to aim at'. It's doubtful whether
Evonne ever felt, or thought, in such banal categories;
she simply *did*.

On her day she was awfully hard to beat, though
Billie Jean King outplayed her in the 1972 Wimbledon final, while the metronomic Chrissie Evert was
too good for her twice in the late seventies. Virginia
Wade beat her in an Australian singles final, which
she did not win till 1974, while for four years in a
row she was runner-up at Forest Hills. It surely did
not perturb her, any more than she seemed much
impressed by the huge sums of money she was making. She was simply, and effortlessly, her own woman.
The tennis circuit did not drive the iron into her
soul as it did to Billie Jean King, nor did it pull her
down to its own brash and mindless level, as it threatened to do to Virginia Wade.

If she was inconsistent, it was not with the passionate, frustrated, self-flagellating anxiety of Virginia
Wade; it was simply because she tended to switch
off. Women's Lib – or Women's Lob, as the tennis
girls' version of it was christened – was of as little
interest to her as to Evert, but for entirely different
reasons. In a very real sense, the tennis world left
her uncorrupted.

Chris Evert, outwardly as imperturbable as Borg,
inwardly quite vulnerable, came from an utterly different background. Blonde and rounded, courteous
to her parents, always perfectly controlled on court,
she seemed the all-American girl, an example to hold
before any tennis-playing daughter. If she loved, lost

and pined for the eternal *enfant terrible*, Jimmy Connors, it was perhaps a question of opposite poles attracting one another. They could scarcely have been more starkly contrasted.

Chris Evert's father, Jimmy, a tennis coach at Fort Lauderdale in Florida, a strong Roman Catholic and a devoted family man with four other handsome children, taught her himself. 'I used to accept Dad's corrections out of fear,' she said in 1972, when she was still only seventeen, 'but our relationship has changed and we've begun to work together as friends. And I agree with a lot of his ideas about religion, curfews and things like that. As for his complaints about little things like long hair or how Notre Dame [the Catholic college] has gotten too liberal, since he went there, I just change the subject and avoid arguments.'

Her astonishing outward poise probably denied her the sympathy and understanding she deserved. In the 1971 Wightman Cup in Cleveland, when she was just about to play, at the age of sixteen, the decisive singles against Virginia Wade, she remarked, 'I notice more sweat than usual on my hands. I must be reacting to the atmosphere.'

She has seldom smiled on court. When she serves she gives little gasps or grunts; a ladylike version of Connors's own. She is quintessentially a baseline player, not remotely as athletic as a Goolagong or as strong as a Navratilova, but remarkable for her steadiness, her tactical sense and her ability to wear down opposition.

Chris Evert's style was never as beguiling as Goolagong's, as dashing as Navratilova's or as aggressive as Billie Jean King's. But you do not pick up a couple of Wimbledon championships and four American singles titles in a row without having something very special to offer. In Evert's case it was her Borg-like concentration, her superb anticipation and the sheer intensity she brought to winning every point. Julie Heldman, her contemporary, wrote: 'She plays points like a siege war in the Middle Ages, hitting hard ground strokes from corner to corner until her opponent is either too tired or too frustrated to keep up the forcing rhythm.' Very seldom indeed did Chris Evert come to the net. Her service, despite the gasp-cum-grunt that accompanied it, was indifferent, her volleying modest, but her two-fisted backhand with its topspin was no mean weapon.

She first won Wimbledon in 1974, beating the Russian Olga Morozova; won it again in 1976, beating Evonne Goolagong, now Cawley; and took the fourth of her American titles when in 1978 the Open was moved to the oven-like Flushing Meadow, which has a surface far less comfortable to her than her beloved clay.

On clay, where long baseline rallies were the thing, she was for a long time unbeatable. By the 1978 U.S. Open, she had not lost a set on clay since 1975 or a match since August 1973. The faster, harder surface gave her opponent, the tall, eighteen-year-old Pam Shriver, an energetic serve-volleyer, much more of a chance, but Miss Evert's sheer consistency prevailed where Miss Navratilova's power had failed. 'I'm sick of tennis,' said Navratilova after her defeat by Pam Shriver.

Chris Evert said that she was tired of it, too, or rather that 'tennis is a business. Pam and Tracy [Austin] will learn that some day'. It had been 'more fun when I was coming up'.

By the same time next year, she had married the

English tennis player John Lloyd and her attitude was
changing. The sheer overpowering will to win which
had been the core of her success had clearly been
eroded. By the early months of 1980 she was losing
matches she would normally have won with ease, and
was even talking about retiring. It was beginning to
seem, as tiny Tracy Austin went from success to
success, that tennis, like gymnastics and swimming,
was a young girl's game, that with growing maturity
came growing boredom, a desire to get off the golden
treadmill and do something else.

Chris Evert Lloyd, after all, had been on the treadmill a very long while. 'Children are the great respon-
sibility of life,' her father has said. 'If you're going
to have them, then you should spend a lot of time with
them. I've done that by having them around the
courts, where I work. I know people say that I've
pushed them, but I don't see it that way. My kids
could have rebelled like some others, but they haven't,
and I think that's because I've made things pleasant
and interesting for them.'

Perhaps. Chris Evert's theme song might almost
have appeared to be 'My Heart Belongs to Daddy',
but a child whose childhood is in some sense taken
away from it tends always to be vulnerable, and often
to react. 'I'm not built as strongly as some of the
women,' Chris once said, 'and I can't be as fluid as
Evonne. So I have to work twice as hard.' Work she
did, but work is not play, even when the work calls
itself tennis. She was very ill prepared for the thousand
natural shocks of her fluctuating engagement to Connors, and when she did find a man who made her
happy it was significant that her tennis at once seemed
to suffer in consequence.

The spectators warmed to her at seventeen, when

she seemed a comforting throw-back to a time before the long-haired, radical, disaffected generation, but in time her very perfection seemed to bore them. None of which affected the fact that she was surely the foremost woman player of her day, precociously mature, whatever the price, and a quietly indomitable competitor.

There has never been anything quiet about Martina Navratilova. She learned English very quickly, and some of the words she learned, and employed on court, were short and Anglo-Saxon. In the early days of her American tours, 'junk' food, consumed in quantity as she drove the freeways, enlarged her already strapping physique until one American journalist wrote that she was built like a Pilsner barrel. She was aggressive, short-tempered, petulant; a magnificent athlete, a left-handed player with a thundering service, a superb volley, and nothing to curb but her own ebullient feelings.

Born and brought up in Revnice, some fifteen miles from Prague, Navratilova was a tomboy who played a wide variety of sports, among them soccer. She first held a tennis racket at the age of five, befriended by a man who later married her mother, to become her stepfather. 'The whole family,' she said when she was eighteen, 'are still playing tennis, even my grandmother. They were all good athletes.'

At eighteen, troubled by the cat-and-mouse behaviour of the Czech authorities and the possibility they might limit her excursions abroad because she was becoming too 'westernized', she made the great leap; she decided to defect. 'At first,' she has said, 'there was a period of emptiness. I didn't know where I belonged. Even now, when I fill out citizenship forms, there is a blank where I have to say "stateless". It makes me feel like a nobody. It makes me feel like a criminal. It makes me doubt myself. Sometimes I wonder if I did the right thing, but I always come to the conclusion that I'm better off where I am.'

Financially, that is unquestionable; she has become very rich. The initial dislocation, however, was traumatic. The joy of breaking through the Iron Curtain, of being in easy-living, welcoming Los Angeles cracked her discipline, lured her into self-indulgence, put pounds on her weight and provoked an orgy of buying: jewels, clothes, shoes.

At the same time, she was extremely vulnerable. Her game was undermined by the way she was living, and the consequent defeats threw her helplessly off-course. 1976 was a deeply disappointing year, and when she was knocked out of the American Open championship at Forest Hills by the Australian Janet Newberry, she wept inconsolably until her eyes were swollen and her voice was hoarse. There was no doubt at all about her talent, her tremendous left-handed serve – which would become better still when she began to slice it – and her adventurous power. There was every doubt about her capacity to exploit it.

Teddy Tinling, more perceptive than he was about Goolagong, remarked, 'As a natural talent, I'm not sure that she's not the best I've ever seen, but natural talents are sometimes the hardest to bridle. When she hasn't pleased herself, she's become petulant and stupid.'

On court, she could seem an overgrown and sulky child. Even when she was right, she could make herself seem in the wrong – as once at Wimbledon when, on the way to the title, Evonne Goolagong broke down with a cry of pain. Far from sympathizing, Martina, television cameras on her, maintained that she herself had been distracted and the point should be hers. The truth was that Evonne, existing on cortisone injections, had no right to be playing at all in such a condition, but Martina made the worst of her case.

Salvation, strangely, lay in a move from Los Angeles to Dallas, Texas, and a friendship with a well-known golfer, Sandra Haynie, who became her companion and her manager. She lost weight, becoming more mobile in consequence, and she began to control the thundering volleys which had been so unpredictable – now exquisite, now erratic. 'I wanted to get away from Los Angeles,' she said. 'I was getting lazy. Life there is so easy that you don't really have to work hard. Everybody makes you welcome and I didn't practise hard enough and was having too good a time to bother with my tennis.'

When she did bother, there was no stopping her. She has won Wimbledon twice and, still in her early twenties, seems likely to be at the top for years to come – even though Chris Lloyd beat her in the semi-final at Wimbledon in 1980. She is still plagued by the phenomenal Tracy Austin but Mrs Lloyd has conceded her crown. 'I suddenly realized,' said Mrs Lloyd, 'that I just didn't care any more. And it's not something I have any control over. I've lost my last three matches to Tracy Austin, and I felt no emotion at all. I used to beat Martina on mental toughness alone, but that intensity is gone, and no one can match her power.'

Evert had admitted when Navratilova was still a

teenager that she was the type of player likely to beat
her: 'Someone strong, aggressive, and a serve-
volleyer.' The point was that to defeat Evert's patient
excellence, you had to be a very *good* serve-volleyer,
and Navratilova was that only intermittently.

In 1978 and 1979 Navratilova's game was not only
powerful but well integrated enough to beat Chris
Evert Lloyd twice in the Wimbledon final. 1978 was
difficult; 1979 immeasurably more easy.

The 1978 final was in the balance till its very last
minutes, when Navratilova ran out at 7–5. The 1979
final was over in an hour, with Chris Evert Lloyd
beaten in straight sets 6–4, 6–4. In 1978 Chris took the
first set 6–2, and it seemed once again that Navratilova's emotions would be her undoing. Instead, she
came boldly back to win the second set 6–4, then, 2–0
down in the third set, drew level at 4–4, and ultimately won. Mrs Lloyd accepted defeat with her cus-
tomary good grace.

The 1979 final was unexpectedly one-sided, given
the fact that only weeks before, at Eastbourne, Mrs
Lloyd had beaten Miss Navratilova in a final set that
went to 15–13. It was a match to treasure, far more
so than the Wimbledon final, with Mrs Lloyd
strangely and most untypically prone to error. She
could never master Navratilova's service, and the
Czech girl scored many winners with her backhand
volleys. The score was 6–4, 6–4, and Navratilova's
mother, grudgingly let out by the Czech government,
was there to see her win.

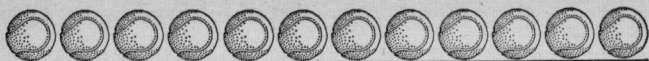

Austin and McEnroe

But it was neither Navratilova nor Lloyd who won the United States Open of 1979 at Flushing Meadow, any more than it was Borg or Connors who won the men's title. It was a little sixteen-year-old called Tracy Austin who beat Mrs Lloyd in the women's final, having beaten Navratilova on the way for good measure; and it was the explosive young John McEnroe who won the men's title.

Not that Lloyd and Navratilova, like Borg and Connors, had not been served due warning. The Young Pretenders had been distinguishing themselves and disconcerting their elders for some time.

A Californian from Rolling Hills, Tracy Austin first played at Wimbledon at the age of fourteen in 1977 – a tiny figure with braces on her teeth, her hair in bunches, insisting on a pocket in her dress because her hand was still too small to hold two tennis balls. She had behind her the familiar Tennis Mother, and a coach, Bob Lansdorp, who had been teaching her since she was six years old. 'My feeling is,' he said, 'that one of the reasons for Tracy's quickness is what I call her eye–foot co-ordination. When she sees where the ball is going, she reacts instantly. She's on her way, ready to meet it, long before it's arrived.'

He had this to say about her double-fisted backhand, which has a force far out of proportion to her size: 'She starts out with her shoulders really turned, and her racket well back, pointing slightly downward from her left hip, the way two-handers do. That's to ensure a low to high swing that will give her what I call at least "the feel of topspin" and keep the ball from sailing out of the court. You'll also notice that her elbows at this point are slightly bent; nothing very exceptional, up to now. But then she gets her hips into it, meets the ball out in front, and rips through it with both of her elbows stiff and both of her arms well extended from her body, not allowing them to hook or to curl at all. And long after the ball is gone, she's still behind it in a free-flowing motion, her elbows still stiff and her arms still extended.'

At fifteen she was already good enough to reach the final of the Virginia Slims tournament in Dallas, beating no less an adversary on the way than Navratilova, who had won her last thirty-seven games. It was in female terms a meeting of David and Goliath. So worried was the big Czech girl by little Tracy's prowess that she was reluctant to follow her service to the net, and paid the penalty. It was a game of immense excitement, Austin winning the first set, Navratilova the second, the third going not only to a tie-break, in which both played stunning shots, but to a deciding point, which Tracy won with a second volley. 'I'm so happy, it's unbelievable, just like a dream,' she said, but more like a dream still was her astonishing victory at Forest Hills the next year.

'It's odd,' said one of her victims in Dallas, the South African, Brigitte Cuypers, 'you don't think she has anything to harm you. She doesn't attack, but she can hit the ball over the net a hundred times if necessary and wait for you to make the error.'

To this extent she resembles Chris Evert Lloyd

rather than Navratilova, but she is very much herself; a unique talent, showing once again the physical democracy of tennis, the ability of the small to stand up to and overcome the large.

John McEnroe has no problems of physique. He is not especially tall at 5 feet 10 inches, but tall enough to produce one of the most dangerous left-handed services the game has ever seen, a serve which not only has tremendous speed, but swerves wickedly away from the player who is receiving it.

McEnroe was born in Wiesbaden where his father, now a successful lawyer, was serving in the U.S. Air Force. The date was 16 February 1959, and four years later the family came back to live in New York. McEnroe was no interloper from the wrong side of the tracks. He was sent to a fashionable New York school called Trinity, even if he preferred a denim jacket to the mandatory coat and tie. He is still not partial to neckwear. At the World Championship Tennis ceremonial lunch, Brian Gottfried observed that it was one of the most remarkable gatherings he had ever attended: John McEnroe was wearing a tie.

Such was his early co-ordination that when, at the age of two, his father was throwing him a ball to hit in a nearby park, a stranger came up to ask whether this was really a child, or a talented midget.

McEnroe's co-ordination is still astonishing. There is no question, in his case, of choosing between the baseline and the net, ground strokes and the serve–volley. He has them all. As Gerulaitis, his fellow New Yorker and victim in the 1979 American final, has said, 'He has so much touch, it's ridiculous.' There are times when the combination of delicacy and power

in his game are such that his racket seems almost to
be a musical instrument.

Yet with the talent goes the temperament; the face,
beneath its bush of hair and red and white headband,
is too often contorted as he shouts at umpires, linesmen or opponents. The nickname Super Brat has
stayed with him. Even his mother has said of him,
'There are times I could just die.' His behaviour is
the more remarkable when one reflects on his upbringing. In social terms, he has nothing to 'prove';
he comes from a prosperous, even an indulgent background. 'I do try to have manners,' he has said. 'I'm
really working on them, not swearing, all that. Maybe
I'm not succeeding so well, but I get so angry with
myself when I play a bad ball. I show it, and there's
nothing much I can do about it.'

In his defence, and that of others like him, it should
be said that there are few games like tennis for gene-
rating such self-disgust, even in the humblest player,
and when the occasion is tense and the money involved
large, it is all the harder to be calm. 'People,' said
McEnroe, 'keep saying I'm nastier than Ilie Nastase,
but it's a different thing with him. I'm very fond of
Ilie, but he really does set out deliberately to upset
people; it's all part of his game. I don't copy him, I
don't aim to annoy people. I just can't help getting
mad with myself.'

Not all his opponents would agree with him; there
have been occasions, not least at Queen's Club in 1978,
when he seemed an unconscionable time re-tying his
laces. Nastase, he once said, 'gets you upset, and sometimes I think, "I don't ever want to speak to this
guy again," but he'll do anything for people, so you
can't stay mad at him long'.

What one might term the shoot-out at the O.K.
Corral came in the 1979 U.S. championships at Flushing Meadow, where the two met in the second round.
Already it was plain that Flushing Meadow was no
Forest Hills in its amenities. Moreover, the crowd
was no ordinary tennis crowd. When the Nastase–
McEnroe game went on as late as 9.45 in the evening,
after a women's match had dragged on for two hours,
many of the spectators were plainly drunk; yet canned
beer was on sale. Oddly the crowd was strongly for
Nastase, and violently against the American.

When they cheered his mistakes, McEnroe, as is his
unfortunate wont, responded in kind, with words
and gestures. What was more, the biter was bitten
when McEnroe slowed the game down by taking the
maximum time between points, and more. (Thirty
seconds is stipulated.) Nastase pretended to go to
sleep behind the baseline, but on the whole he was
exceedingly good-tempered.

Frank Hammond, a leading umpire, kept rebuking
Nastase through a live microphone, which made the
crowd even more restless. When he penalized Nastase
a game there was chaos, with catcalls and a volley
of beer cans. The match was held up for seventeen
minutes, Nastase was disqualified by the tournament
referee, reinstated by Bill Talbert, the tournament
director, and finally beaten in four sets. McEnroe
went on to beat first Jimmy Connors, then the blond
Gerulaitis, an extremely talented fellow New Yorker
with a penchant for the good life and expensive cars.
McEnroe was the youngest American champion since
Pancho Gonzales; abundant consolation for going out
early at Wimbledon to Gullikson – again to the delight of a crowd which did not like him.

McEnroe would clearly like to be liked, but finds it more important to win. He has cogent things to say about umpiring. 'I'm not denying they might love tennis, and that's fine, but it's a fact that older people don't see as well as younger people. You can't expect an old umpire to pick up a fast serve as quickly as a younger person and they're going to make mistakes: that's obvious. The average age of an umpire is probably sixty or so. I mean, it's absurd.' In such remarks, he was merely echoing what such other Americans as Gonzales himself and Gardnar Mulloy had said about umpires; not least those at Wimbledon, where line judges have been known to fall asleep in the sun.

'People,' said McEnroe, 'say the faces [pulled on court] are bad temperament compared to Borg. When I question a call, some people don't like that; pure tennis nuts, or whatever. Maybe they're right, and maybe they're wrong, but if everyone was like Stan Smith or Arthur Ashe – you know, showing no emotion – I don't think tennis would be as exciting as it is or as big, either. There have got to be personalities on the court. I just have a pretty fiery personality when I play and I don't think there will be rule-makers who try to take that away from me.'

The rate of his progress has been extraordinary, even if he did fall in Buenos Aires in the 1980 Davis Cup. Giving up a law course at Stanford University, he entered the Wimbledon qualifying tournament of 1978 as an eighteen-year-old, won his way through, and went on to the semi-final proper. 1979 may have seen him upset at Wimbledon, but he won not only Forest Hills but the Masters and the World Championship Tennis titles.

Harry Hopman, the Australian who once coached

him, has said of McEnroe, 'Johnny is strong-willed, not brash. There's a difference. There's never been a champion who hasn't been strong-willed or determined to assert himself in his own style. Sometimes Johnny's style is blunt. He disagrees. But he is surrounded by older people – most of his opponents, and the officials – and he feels he must stand up for himself at times. A brash person is loutish, and Johnny is not. But he is a kid from New York City, and I have found that such youngsters will speak out.'

From New York City, you will notice – like Gerulaitis – and not from California. The pendulum had swung, the catchment area had radically extended. 'Sure he's a New Yorker,' said an American writer called John Powers, 'which explains some of the cockiness. But he's not the tough New York kid he acts at times. He went to a good prep school and grew up with money. But because of this I think he tries twice as hard not to act as a preppie or let anybody push him around just because he comes from the right side of town. The gentleman stuff in tennis rubs him the wrong way.' The analysis may well be correct, though nonetheless ironical for all that. Connors and McEnroe, the underprivileged and the privileged, meeting on a plateau of intransigence, each for his own differing reasons.

McEnroe may be slim, but he is extremely strong and a splendid doubles player – not least in partnership with Peter Fleming – as well as a superb singles player. He was the first younger player ever to beat Borg – in Stockholm at that, in November 1978 – and Borg said plaintively afterwards that he wanted to attack McEnroe's weakness but he could not find one.

'Against Connors and Borg,' said Arthur Ashe –

who, poor fellow, suffered a heart attack in 1979 – 'you feel like you're being hit with a sledgehammer. But this guy is a stiletto. Junior has great balance and he just slices people up. He's got a ton of shots. It's slice here, nick there, cut over here. Pretty soon you've got blood all over you, even though the wounds aren't deep. Soon after that, you've bled to death.'

Jimmy Connors, in the semi-final of the 1979 U.S. Open, and Gerulaitis, in the final itself, must have found the experience rather more akin to being dismembered with a machete. Thriving in the polluted heat of his native city on the difficult rubberized-acrylic green surface, McEnroe simply annihilated both of them. Borg had long since fallen by the way-side to the ferocious serving of Roscoe Tanner – and an accompanying dirge from his coach Lennart Bergelin: 'Is not tennis, is not tennis. Cannot see at night.'

McEnroe appeared to have no trouble. His serves were wickedly effective, and he was mustard at the net. Connors went down in straight sets, as he had in Lamar Hunt's W. C. T. championships in Dallas, and declared afterwards he had a bad back. Gerulaitis made no such excuse as he too went to the wall in straight sets: 7–5, 6–3, 6–3. 'It isn't every day that two players who live ten minutes from the Open reach the final,' McEnroe declared. 'New Yorkers should appreciate this. It may never happen again.' Gerulaitis, who had won a thrilling semi-final against Tanner, coming back from a two-set deficit, could not cope with McEnroe's serve, nor make much of his volleying, his wristy backhand, and his periodic, teasing drop shots.

McEnroe's supremacy, however, was short-lived as

Borg beat him in a thrilling final at Wimbledon in 1980 to take his fifth consecutive title – a staggering feat. Borg dropped the first set 1–6, won the next two, dropped the fourth on a nerve-wracking tie-break, and eventually won the fifth 8–6 on the last of eight match points. His achievement became the more remarkable when it was made known that he had suffered since his first match of the tournament from the agony of a torn stomach muscle. A champion indeed. McEnroe, however, had a spectacular revenge over Borg in the final of the American championships in Flushing Meadow the following September.

As for Tracy Austin's performance in the 1979 U.S. Open, she proved once again in her semi-final with Navratilova that bulk is not enough, and showed herself in the final still more consistent than even Chris Evert Lloyd. Even Robert Lansdorp, Tracy's coach, was surprised. She had almost lost her fourth-round match against Kathy Jordan, which went to three sets and a tie-breaker, and when the semi-final was postponed a day for television's sake, he exploited the hiatus to work intensely with her on her basic strokes and show her how to combat Navratilova's swinging service. Out she came to defeat Navratilova, though she had beaten her before only four times out of fifteen, started with a double fault, and was almost at once pulverized by a sizzling forehand.

What Miss Austin has besides her skill, however, is colossal courage, and she hung on to vary her shots, run into a 5–2 lead and eventually take the set at 7–5, after slipping to 5–5 and love–forty on her own serve. The second set went to her by the same score, Navratilova maintaining her strangely negative streak.

As for the final, Chris Lloyd, who had beaten Billie Jean King – fresh from yet another operation – with absolute ease, seemed favourite. She had lost fifteen pounds in weight and the metronome seemed to be ticking away superbly. But it was Chris Lloyd who made mistakes at crucial moments, and little Austin, youngest player ever to win the tournament, who stayed serene.

Mrs Lloyd was 4–3 ahead in the first set when, on her own service, she missed an easy overhead shot, dropped the game and eventually went down 6–4. The second set was Tracy Austin's at 6–3. Robert Lansdorp, so sure she would lose that he had promised to give up smoking if she won, found himself held to his vow.

At the 1980 Wimbledon championship, however, the roles were reversed and Tracy Austin was defeated in the semi-final by Mrs Lloyd. In that year, too, a champion of the future was surely to be seen in the pigtailed 15-year-old, Andrea Jaeger, daughter of a tennis coach, who knocked out the eternally fluctuating Virginia Wade. The title went to the popular Evonne Cawley, after a most unusual nine-year gap, her victim in the final being Chris Lloyd. Both had married English players and it seemed to have done them no harm.

Tennis, then, has not only survived and developed triumphantly since its origins in Victorian England; it continues to grow in popularity at a speed which any other sport might envy. With extraordinarily little change in rules, and none at all in living memory in the shape of the court, it has proved itself as acceptable to this frantic age as it was to the more leisurely one which produced it. It is perhaps the most truly international of all major sports, and it does not seem even yet to have reached its zenith among either players or spectators.

Like any great sport, it seems to possess, despite its basic simplicity, an infinite capacity for change and surprise. Thus if the serve-and-volley game seemed to have brushed the baseline game aside, here is Bjorn Borg, the greatest player yet known, who operates largely from the baseline. If open professionalism has brought faults in its wake, they are largely the faults of the society around it which tennis must inevitably reflect. Those faults cannot obscure its enormous basic vitality.

Index

More non fiction in Puffins

The Puffin Book of Athletics

Neil Allen

Packed with useful information about the great races and great athletes. With a foreword by Olympic gold medallist, Sebastian Coe.

The Puffin Book of Sewing

Jackie Andrews

The basic techniques to make home sewing simple and enjoyable.

Aidan Chambers' Book of Ghosts and Hauntings

Spooky houses and tall tales – a serious investigation into the unknown.

Forgers

Lance Salway

A narrative of famous fakes, frauds and forgeries, illustrated with photographs throughout.

Heard about the Puffin Club?

... it's a way of finding out more about Puffin books
and authors, of winning prizes (in competitions), sharing
jokes, a secret code, and perhaps seeing your name in
print! When you join you get a copy of our magazine,
Puffin Post, sent to you four times a year, a badge and a
membership book.

For details of subscription and an application form, send
a stamped addressed envelope to:

The Puffin Club Dept A
Penguin Books Limited
Bath Road
Harmondsworth
Middlesex UB7 0DA

and if you live in Australia, please write to:

The Australian Puffin Club
Penguin Books Australia Limited
P.O. Box 257
Ringwood
Victoria 3134